POPULAR IN HEAVEN FAMOUS IN HELL

R. T. KENDALL

CHARISMA HOUSE

Most Charisma House Book Group products are available at special quantity discounts for bulk purchase for sales promotions, premiums, fund-raising, and educational needs. For details, write Charisma House Book Group, 600 Rinehart Road, Lake Mary, Florida 32746, or telephone (407) 333-0600.

Popular in Heaven, Famous in Hell by R. T. Kendall
Published by Charisma House
Charisma Media/Charisma House Book Group
600 Rinehart Road
Lake Mary, Florida 32746
www.charismahouse.com

Visit the author's website at www.rtkendallministries.com.

Library of Congress Cataloging-in-Publication Data

Names: Kendall, R. T., 1935- author.
Title: Popular in heaven, famous in hell / R.T. Kendall.
Description: Lake Mary, Florida : Charisma House, 2018. | Includes bibliographical references.
Identifiers: LCCN 2018013375 (print) | LCCN 2018032272 (ebook) | ISBN
9781629995526 (ebook) | ISBN 9781629995519 (trade paper)
Subjects: LCSH: Christian life.
Classification: LCC BV4501.3 (ebook) | LCC BV4501.3 .K456 2018 (print) | DDC
248.4--dc23
LC record available at https://lccn.loc.gov/2018013375

An application to register this book for cataloging has been submitted to the Library of Congress.
International Standard Book Number: 978-1-62999-551-9
E-book ISBN: 978-1-62999-552-6

18 19 20 21 22 — 987654321
Printed in the United States of America

To Bill and Shirley

Only one life, `twill soon be past;
Only what's done for Christ will last.

If Jesus Christ be God and died for me, then no sacrifice can be too great for me to make for Him.

Some want to live within the sound
Of church or chapel bell;
I want to run a rescue shop,
Within a yard of hell.

—C. T. Studd (1862–1931)

CONTENTS

FOREWORD

IF YOU ARE wanting easy solutions or something to make you comfortable in your Christian life, then put this book down! This book is dangerous for those who want to remain in their comfort zones. It will shake you to your foundation! It did me.

Dr. R.T. Kendall is one of my five top favorite preachers/teachers. "Why?" you might ask, especially when you learn I met him only a little over a year ago. I'll tell you why. I heard him preach on the subject of "How to Forgive Yourself Totally"—something that has been difficult for me and a subject I returned to time and again. I listened to him as he shared his own struggle with the issue. I was captured by his transparency and the ease with which he approached the subject. Not that it was easy, but he put me at ease because I sensed in him a fellow pilgrim, someone who knew what it was like to carry a burden for which it seemed impossible to forgive yourself.

Dr. Kendall, or R.T., as he insists I call him, has wonderful scholarly credentials (Oxford) and great experiences (Westminster Chapel in London)—"top drawer" as some might say. But he is eminently practical. He lives where you and I do—in the trenches of life. And he is honest about real-life struggles. He doesn't just slap a Bible verse over an issue or give platitudes. No. He takes us straight into the Word of God, making us hungry for more. He ushers us into the very throne room to get the wisdom we crave for living life. He makes complicated theological truths understandable for you and me. He "puts the hay down where the cows can get it"! Yet he never compromises the transcendence of God.

The book you hold in your hand is an important "primer" for living the Christian life—one that honors God. It's not just for a new Christian but for old ones, like me, who have been travelling the road for a long time but need a good swift kick to move us on. It will become a classic you'll want to read and reread. This book will challenge you to be popular in heaven and famous in hell. I pray to be like that.

—Ruth Graham
Ruth Graham Ministries
Best-Selling Author, *In Every Pew Sits a Broken Heart*

FOREWORD

THIS BOOK ARRIVED in my life at exactly the right moment. Perhaps I might not have been so keen to open it if I'd known how hard it was going to hit me! So be warned if you are looking for a kindly God to keep you healthy and make life easy, comfortable, and prosperous—don't bother to open it. Yet I can promise you, if you do dare, you will come away with a far bigger God than you've ever encountered before.

It was thirty years ago when I first met R. T. We were on a conference platform in Bristol, England; he was the celebrity speaker, and I was just there to give a short warm-up testimony. I was speechless with awe as he towered over my wheelchair. I had spent countless hours listening to his teaching tapes after becoming disabled by encephalitis.

A few years later when God healed me completely and lastingly through the prayers of a new Christian, R. T. was hugely supportive. The story of my sudden healing upset a lot of prominent Christians who felt that miracles only happened in Bible times, and I was labeled a fraud in leading Christian newspapers. I was bewildered because I knew for certain God had done something for me that no human could do. R. T.'s very public support and encouragement meant a great deal to me, and his book *Total Forgiveness* showed me what to do with all my critics!

Ever since then I've been working for the Lord in the healing ministry—and so has the girl who prayed for me back in 1990. But life in ministry is never easy, and the year that led up to R. T.'s request for me to write this foreword has been exceptionally difficult. I think I had hit what he describes in the book as a "betrayal barrier." I felt God had let me down by allowing several things to happen in my life and work. If He really loved me as passionately and intimately as I thought, "Then how could He allow life to be so tough?" Unanswered prayers and thwarted hopes were making me secretly resentful and full of grumbles and complaints. Surely after years of working for Him I deserved better treatment than this.

As I read this book, I realized that every single one of God's servants has faced a similar faith crisis and had to choose to go on trusting God even when He felt distant, disinterested, and unable to keep His promises.

R. T. took me right up above the world and let me see both hell and heaven from God's perspective. It was gloriously soul expanding!

R. T. has gathered together all the treasures of wisdom he has collected over sixty years in ministry, and he has made them accessible to the rest of us. Thank you, R. T.!

—JENNIFER REES LARCOMBE
BEAUTY FROM ASHES

PREFACE

THE TITLE OF this book owes its origin to two old friends—both of whom are in heaven. First, John Paul Jackson (1950–2015). Best known for his prophetic gift and needed emphasis on the priority of character over gifting, John Paul once made a comment to me, which I'll reveal in chapter 1, that became the foundation for the first part of this book.

Second, Rolfe Barnard (1904–1969) was one of my early mentors. A rugged, old-fashioned Southern Baptist preacher, he helped refine my theology and preaching style. In 1963 he preached an amazing sermon, "A Man Who Was Known in Hell," based on Acts 19:15. That sermon became the springboard for the second half of this book.

I dedicate this book to Dr. and Mrs. Wilmer Kerns. Dedicating a book to them is long overdue. Bill Kerns was my very close friend at Trevecca Nazarene University in Nashville many years ago. I will never forget the day of my experience with the Holy Spirit on October 31, 1955. He saw me across the Trevecca campus and came to my dormitory room in Tidwell Hall to ask, "What has happened to you?" I replied: "Something has happened, but I don't know what it is." He quizzed me that day in a manner that started a process of enabling me to see for myself what actually happened. From that day to this he has helped shape my thinking and has remained a loyal friend and confidant.

I am hugely indebted to Ruth Graham and Jennifer Rees Larcombe for their respective forewords for American and British readers. I am grateful to Barbara Dycus for her editorial skills.

Thank you, Steve and Joy Strang, for your encouragement. My deepest thanks as always is to my wife, Louise—my best friend and critic.

—R. T. Kendall
January 2018
Hendersonville, Tennessee

PART I

POPULAR IN HEAVEN

And without faith it is impossible to please God, because anyone who comes to him must believe that he exists and that he rewards those who earnestly seek him.

—HEBREWS 11:6

Chapter 1

BEING WELL CONNECTED

When they saw the courage of Peter and John and realized that they were unschooled, ordinary men, they were astonished and they took note that these men had been with Jesus.

—Acts 4:13

Would you like to be famous? If honest, most of us would. But famous where? What if you walked into a party in Buckingham Palace and as you entered, you overheard the queen whisper to the person she was speaking to: "Oh look it's . . . "? Or perhaps you imagine listening in on a conversation in the Oval Office and hear the president mention your name: "Oh yes, I know . . . He/She is quite something!" Would that make you feel good? Or how about this: imagine there is a meeting in hell—millions of demons are present and the devil himself is working the room. Suddenly you hear him mention a name—your name. At first you are surprised—even a little afraid. But then you remember that some other names are known there too. The demon said to the imposter in Acts 19:15: "Jesus I know, and Paul

I know about, but who are you?" And suddenly you realize something that at last convinces you that your life has made a difference in the battle between good and evil. You are one of a select group: you are famous in hell.

Being famous in hell is quite something. But on its own it's not enough. John Paul Jackson was best known for his prophetic gift. He and I became close friends. One day I phoned him to say, "I have a sermon for a church this Sunday, but I don't think it will be very popular with them."

He replied: "Will it be popular in heaven? If it will be popular in heaven, that's the only thing that matters."

My dear reader, life is short. The things that grasp our attention now will one day seem like mere trinkets. Every day we breathe in and out—in and out—thousands of times a day. There is a day fixed, that unless Jesus comes first, you and I will only breathe *out*. No amount of money, power, or prestige can alter the date that we each have with death. And at that moment the only thing that will matter is whether we have known Christ and served Him well—that our lives have made a difference. In short: that we are popular in heaven—and famous in hell.

Recently an old classmate of 1953 from Ashland High School in Kentucky loaned me his copy of the annual, which contains photographs of all the students of that year and write-ups and photos of the more popular students at the time. It was both fun and sobering. Fun to see what I looked like then as well as old friends I have not seen in many years. Sobering because these photos brought me right back to those days when I was conscious of being not very popular. My former church teaching prohibited me from attending cinemas and school dances. I was never "in" with the popular students. My photo is found only when I was in a group such as with the high school band.

Popularity in school was of paramount importance—then. Oh yes. Peer pressure dominated how one felt. You dressed not to be criticized. You dressed in a manner that might bring compliments. You spoke when it would be accepted by those who heard you. You did not always consciously think about it, but you wanted to be liked. You wanted to be "in." There was a time when I cared more about what my parents thought. But at some stage their views and approval were pretty much eclipsed by what my classmates in school thought. What fellow students thought became more important than what my parents thought, what my pastor thought, or what any authority figure thought. What mattered was what those of my age thought. It was totally embarrassing not to go to the cinema or the school dances. Even buying a class ring was out of the question; it was regarded as "worldly" by my church. But peer relationships were what seemed so important.

If only I could have realized then how *little* these things would mean one day! When I preach to young people nowadays I try to make this point. I'm not sure whether many take it in. The influence of peer pressure on young people is so great. It controls so many decisions they make, who they go out with, who they are seen with. One day these influences will mean *nothing*.

Not only that, it was very revealing when I discovered where those most popular students are today—who succeeded in life, how many had happy marriages, where they lived, and what their values are today. The funny thing is, with few exceptions, those who were most popular then are almost entirely forgotten now—even if still alive. The ones who were regarded as most likely to succeed became virtually unknown. And then I think how important they seemed then!

An Even More Sobering Truth

These things said, I blush to admit that I have not changed much in the past seventy years! My initial reaction in my life and ministry is still based upon "what they think." I am ashamed to say that I still think of the same things—what my friends and foes might think or say, whether what I preach or write will be applauded; will it make new enemies or will it endear me to those who already accept me?

During my twenty-five years at Westminster Chapel—the "best of times, the worst of times" to quote Charles Dickens (1812–1870)—I was conscious that all I said publicly was being tape-recorded to go around the world. There were those in the congregation with their notepads—waiting with glee for any unguarded comment they might quote and, hopefully, regard as heresy. It was hard not to think of people like that when preparing a sermon.

Here is my consolation when I contemplate my embarrassing weakness after these seventy years: there is a difference between temptation and sin. I thank God for this distinction. I am embarrassed by what tempts me—to be popular on this earth—but I remember that Jesus was tempted as we are. He did not sin (Heb. 4:15). The question is: Do we accept the grim reality of what tempts us and reject this temptation? Or do we give in to it?

We do not outgrow temptation in this life, no matter how spiritual, godly, experienced, or seasoned we become. Neither will we be perfectly like Jesus on this earth. Paul admitted that he wasn't perfect yet (Phil. 3:13). That is what glorification is for!

Jesus never outgrew temptation. He was tested to the hilt right up to the final moment of His death on the cross. Partly what kept Him focused was that the reward was worth waiting for. "For the joy set before him" Jesus "endured the cross" and scorned "its shame" (Heb. 12:2).

Therefore we must learn to *resist* temptation. That includes the temptation for someone like me to write or preach what will please the readers or hearers.

You may not be a writer or a preacher. But keep reading. Do you not have the temptation to be well received here on earth? Do you not hope what you wear, say, or do will be acceptable to your friends? Do you make *spiritual* decisions based upon what people will think of you?

I would hate to think that God was at work right under my nose and yet I might miss it because I value my reputation.

Rolfe Barnard loved to quote Jonathan Edwards' (1703–1758) conviction that the task of every generation is to discover in which direction the Sovereign Redeemer is moving, then move in that direction.

So often people miss the work of the Spirit for one reason: what their friends will think if they follow the Holy Spirit. One might even miss their calling in life owing to displeasing a friend or an authority figure.

Are you like that? Would you risk your reputation in order to find out what is pleasing to God? Or is what "they" think more important to you?

Is being popular important to you? Being famous? Being well connected?

The early disciples were derided. But they were famous for having been with Jesus. Being well connected like that is as good as it gets.

That is what this book is about.

Chapter 2

THE FLEETING PRIVILEGE OF FAITH

For before he [Enoch] was taken, he was commended as one who pleased God.

—Hebrews 11:5

Faith is a fleeting privilege. Now is the time to believe. Now is the time to please God. You will not always have this privilege. Have you ever come to the place where you appreciate the privilege of faith? Do you not realize it is a fleeting privilege? You will not always be able to believe, that is, to believe without seeing.

Given the atheistic definition of faith—seeing is believing—I can promise you this: you *will* one day "see and believe." You really will. "'Look, he is coming with the clouds,' and '*every eye will see him*, even those who pierced him'; and all peoples on earth 'will mourn because of him'" (Rev. 1:7, emphasis added). Some translate the word for "mourn" as *wail.* It will be the most awful sound ever heard. The pathos of a wail cannot be described in words. I only heard it once—many years ago. I will never forget it. When all men and women see that they missed it forever they will wail. They will then see that Jesus Christ is the eternal

Son of God—God in the flesh—who died on the cross and was raised from the dead. This will happen when the rich and the poor, the sophisticated and the simple, the aristocracy and the common man *wail.* Scream. All because it will be absolutely too late. Eternally too late.

Oh yes, they will "believe" then. They will see. But it will be too late for true faith. The rich man "believed" in *Hades.* He prayed. "Send Lazarus to dip the tip of his finger in water and cool my tongue, because I am in agony in this fire" (Luke 16:24). But such a prayer will never be answered.

This is why it's so critical that we choose faith now while we still have time. The question we should all be asking ourselves is: What makes us popular in heaven? Answer: faith. "Without faith it is impossible to please God" (Heb. 11:6). Enoch had this witness before his translation into heaven—that he "pleased God" (v. 5).

That is the greatest thing that can ever be said about a person on this earth: that he or she *pleased God.* It is the greatest accomplishment, the greatest achievement, and the greatest attainment that a human being ever did. Greater than being a multibillionaire, greater than climbing Mount Everest, greater than receiving the Nobel Peace Prize, and greater than being elected to the highest office in any nation is to have it said of you that you *pleased God.* You can do this without being prime minister or president. It must be said also that you can be a head of state and have the acclaim and adulation of the people and displease God. King Saul had power, authority, and the admiration of the people when he was in fact rejected by God (1 Sam. 16:1). Sadly the importance of pleasing God seems to escape the plans of the high and mighty of this world. Jesus asked a simple question: "What good is it for someone to gain the whole world, yet forfeit their soul?" (Mark 8:36).

Pleasing God is done one way: by faith. *Faith* is "confidence in what we hope for and assurance about what we do not see" (Heb.

11:1). This definition of faith goes right against the view of the secular atheist who says, "Seeing is believing." The atheist says, "I will believe it when I see it." The problem with this is, it is not faith in that case. Faith to be *faith* that is being exercised must be believed without seeing. Those who crucified Jesus said, "Let this Messiah, this king of Israel, come down now from the cross, that we may *see and believe*" (Mark 15:32, emphasis added). That is the rationale of the secular person today—they want to *see* in order to believe. But what they would "believe" after this seeing could not be graced with the title "faith." For faith, in the Bible, to be faith is to believe without seeing.

The people in Hebrews 11 accomplished great things by faith—by believing without seeing. "The world was not worthy of them," says the writer (Heb. 11:38). That brings us to one of the essential ingredients to being popular in heaven, namely, that we may not be popular on the earth. It does not mean we will never be popular in some sense. But if Hebrews 11 is a gauge for what is popular in heaven, it is likely to come in proportion to whether we are *unpopular on earth*—if it is owing to our faith that makes us unpopular. According to Hebrews 11:38, the world is not worthy of those who are unpopular on earth owing to their faith. Yes, the world is not worthy of such people. Such people are despised by the world. This is because you cannot focus on pleasing God and pleasing people at the same time. You must make a choice—it is either the aim to please God alone or maintain the applause of people.

Being popular in heaven will not make you popular on earth. That is, while you are alive. They may praise you after you are gone! Yes. That was what the Pharisees did. They praised the prophets of old. They, like all Jews, extolled the prophets of a previous generation—and blamed their forefathers for rejecting them. The Pharisees in Jesus' day were very religious Jews who thought they were without sin and who kept the Mosaic Law.

They were the chief enemies of Jesus. They did not realize that by rejecting Jesus they were being no different from their forefathers who rejected the prophets. Their forefathers hated the ancient prophets—whether it was Samuel or Isaiah. But after the prophets were dead, they became heroes! Worse still, the Pharisees so lacked objectivity about themselves that they fancied they would have been different from those who killed the prophets had they been alive, say, in Isaiah's day. When the writer of Hebrews said that some people were "sawed in two" (Heb. 11:37), he was referring to Isaiah. Isaiah was tortured and killed by their forefathers. But the Pharisees—who would claim to extol Isaiah—said: "If *we* had lived in the days of our ancestors, *we* would not have taken part with them in shedding the blood of the prophets" (Matt. 23:30, emphasis added). In other words, the Pharisees believed they were a cut above their forefathers. Jesus said they were no different. They proved this by the way they hated Jesus.

Jesus made it plain to the disciples that we will be hated in our generation, but added, "If the world hates you, keep in mind that it hated me first" (John 15:18). In other words, the world hated Jesus, and if we are truly followers of Jesus the world will hate us. Or as Paul put it, all who live godly in Christ Jesus will suffer persecution (2 Tim. 3:12).

By the way, Jesus' words that the world hated Him first are a reminder that people who claim to admire Jesus today don't have a clue who He was or what He was like.

We all like to think that we would not have crucified Jesus. The Pharisees and the religious Jews crucified Jesus, but we would not do such a thing! The truth is, you and I crucified Jesus. It was our sins that put Him on the cross. But those who have not come to be convicted of sin suppose Jesus to be a good and wonderful man. They fancy that they see integrity, goodness, and virtue in Jesus that the Pharisees did not see. People who have not been convicted of sin think like that. They suppose that had they been living in Jesus' day with the power the Jews had, Jesus would not have been crucified.

Wrong. Totally wrong. Once the blindness on our minds as to who Jesus is and what He did is removed, we will either love Him or hate Him. If the Holy Spirit quickens us to see our sinfulness, we will love Him. If left to ourselves without the Spirit's effectual calling, we will hate Him. Jesus did not pretend that all would follow Him. He knew that some would, some wouldn't. "All those the Father gives me *will* come to me" (John 6:37, emphasis added). In other words, whatever number of people that the Father gave to Jesus would be the number who would follow Him. If that number included every person who was ever born, then every person who was ever born would follow Jesus! But not every person who was ever born was given to Jesus by the Father. Why? I don't know. God does not tell us why. I recently heard Kathy Keller, wife of Dr. Tim Keller, share her life verse. She did this in the light of the discussion regarding God's purpose to save some but not all. She therefore adopted this verse for truths we do not understand: "The secret things belong to the LORD our God, but the things revealed belong to us and to our children forever, that we may follow all the words of this law" (Deut. 29:29). For this reason Paul could say, "We are to God the pleasing aroma of Christ among those who are being saved and those who are perishing" (2 Cor. 2:15). But those who are perishing are those who, like the ancient Pharisees, hate Jesus Christ.

My old pastor Henry Mahan used to say, "When the pure gospel is preached to men as they are, it will save some and condemn others, but it will accomplish God's purpose."

Affirming God's Sovereignty

We must make up our minds that not everybody will be saved. We must nonetheless try to save them. We should try to reach every living person with the gospel—and try to convert them as if their destiny were determined by us. The same God who said, "I will have mercy on whom I have mercy" (Rom. 9:15), also said, "Go into all the world and preach the gospel to all creation" (Mark 16:15). It is obedience to and affirmation of the *whole* Word of God that will make us popular in heaven. It is obedience to affirm the teaching of the sovereignty of God; it is equally obedience to try to save the world. But we cannot change their wills. We can twist their arms. And I would even say we should gently twist their arms until they say *no*. But we cannot change their hearts. Only God can do that. This is why Jesus said, "No one can come to me unless the Father who sent me draw them" (John 6:44, 65).

What pleases God in this instance, then, is that we are faithful to Him in seeking to save the lost. This will make us popular in heaven. Do you want to be popular in heaven? Become a soul winner. As C. T. Studd put it, rescue people a yard away from hell.

What pleases God, then, is that we affirm His sovereignty—His right to save whom He will—and equally fulfill the Great Commission to reach the whole world. It is my view that those who uphold evangelism and the sovereignty of God simultaneously are popular in heaven. Don't try to figure it out. Moses, to whom I will refer further below, tried to figure out how a bush could be ablaze and not be consumed. God said, "Stop! Don't come any closer. You are on holy ground." (See Exodus 3:5.) Bringing together God's glorious sovereignty and robust evangelism is pleasing to God. But it is holy ground on which we are not allowed to walk with shoes on. We walk on holy ground barefooted. Walking barefooted takes humility—the willingness not to understand everything fully. To put it another way, the distinction between God's sovereign will and man's utter responsibility is holy ground. We cannot walk on holy ground until we take off our shoes. Then in humility we worship. We must not try to get too close to grasping how a bush on fire is not consumed. We must keep our distance. We worship God barefooted in deepest humility. "The secret things belong to the LORD our God" (Deut. 29:29).

BE WILLING NOT TO KNOW EVERYTHING

Don't try to figure everything out! That is partly what makes faith, *faith.* We will never come to faith by understanding certain truths first; it is our faith—believing God—that seeks understanding. God will always tell us what we truly *need* to know. Additionally, He will often tell us what we *want* to know, but only if and when we are truly ready. This readiness will come little by little, and it doesn't mean we will understand everything there is to know about God before we get to heaven.

> "For my thoughts are not your thoughts,
> neither are your ways my ways,"
> declares the LORD.
> "As the heavens are higher than the earth,
> so are my ways higher than your ways
> and my thoughts than your thoughts."
>
> —ISAIAH 55:8–9

Until He makes things perfectly clear to us, believe the ABCs of God's Word. Jesus said that he who is faithful in that which is least will be faithful also in much (Luke 16:10). God makes things clear to us one step at a time. Until He makes Himself totally clear—which He will do on the day of judgment—let us believe Him without getting all our questions answered in advance.

This is what will make us popular in heaven. As we will see below, those valiant people described in Hebrews 11 did not get all their questions answered. But by believing what was promised, they turned the world upside down.

Faith, then, is believing God. This is the definition Dr. Martyn Lloyd-Jones, my greatest mentor, gave me many years ago. Faith is believing what He says. Believing His Word. Holding fast to His Word whether we fully grasp it or whether we have success on earth or not.

What pleases Him? Our persistence in upholding His integrity. The Bible is God's integrity put on the line. Our integrity must be an unwavering faith in His Word, however unpopular it may be with people on the earth.

Two Kinds of Faith

There are two kinds of biblical faith: saving faith and persistent faith. Either of these makes you popular in heaven. Saving faith is what gets you to heaven; it is the repentance that brings joy in the presence of the angels (Luke 15:10). It is when you say to God: "I am sorry for my sins. I transfer my reliance upon good works to what Jesus did for me on the cross." That is the faith that saves. Hebrews 11, however, is not about saving faith; it is about persistent faith.

Persistent faith is what makes you popular in heaven by believing God and not being motivated by popularity on earth. If you insist on being popular on earth, you will be unpopular in heaven. If you want to be popular in heaven, you must abandon your quest to be approved by people on earth. I'm sorry, but you cannot have it both ways.

That said, one must admit that sometimes God will give you a measure of popularity on earth *if that was not your motive.* If your motive is to please God—and God alone—and some people still admire you, fine. God may allow that. He does that at times. When I am at a low point—and I have been there many, many times—sometimes God causes somebody to give an encouraging word that will lift me up. But if popularity on earth is your *aim*, you choose to forfeit the honor that would have come to you from God.

The God of the Bible is a jealous God (Exod. 34:14). Like it or not, that is the way He is. That is His nature. This will never change. Moreover, in order to be popular in heaven, you must come to terms with God's jealousy. And approve of it. Accept it. And come to love it.

Which is what Oprah Winfrey has so far chosen not to do. Many years ago she sadly turned her back on her evangelical background when she heard her pastor say that God is a jealous God. Oprah did not like this; she wanted to live her own life. She resented a God who wanted total control over her. She made her decision and never looked back.[1] She became arguably the most popular person on the earth! But as Yogi Berra (1925–2015) put it, "It ain't over till it's over." Like most people, I admire Oprah Winfrey. She is amazing. But I would not want to be in her shoes for anything in the world. Eternity lasts a long time.

The Side of the Angels

The question all of us should ask is this: What is popular in heaven? If it is popular in heaven, I choose to be on the side of the angels! And the sainted dead!

Apart from the triune God—Father, Son, and Holy Spirit—there are two categories of beings in heaven: the angels of various descriptions and the sainted dead (Heb. 12:22–23).

The angels exist for the glory and pleasure of God. The angels in heaven are those beings who did *not* fall at some point in time before the creation of the world. Paul calls these "elect angels" (1 Tim. 5:21). Never forget that certain angels revolted in heaven. They were those who "did not keep their positions of authority but abandoned their proper dwelling." They were "kept in darkness, bound with everlasting chains for judgment on the great Day" (Jude 6). God did not spare the angels that sinned, but "sent them to hell [Greek Tartarus], putting them into gloomy dungeons to be held for judgment" (2 Pet. 2:4).

You can be sure that Satan, also known as "Lucifer, son of

the morning" (Isa. 14:12, KJV), "morning star, son of the dawn," sought to recruit every angel in the created universe to join with him in his revolt against God. How many revolted? Possibly one-third of them. (See Revelation 12:4.) However many there were that sinned, there were those that did not sin—that did not revolt. Those are the angels that are in heaven now. They are accomplished in spiritual warfare. They resisted Satan.

These angels please God.

Such angels are perfect worshippers of God. They do not want any worship of themselves or even attention from us (Rev. 19:10; 22:9). You cannot bribe them, you cannot get them to do things for you; they are focused entirely, absolutely, and perfectly on pleasing God. Jesus spoke of "rejoicing in the presence of the angels of God over one sinner who repents" (Luke 15:10). This suggests that there are things on earth that make the angels rejoice. Not that they will convey their rejoicing to us. But we may assume they do rejoice when things on earth are done according to the will of God.

Nor should we conceive from this that we should try to please angels. We are to please God. And God alone. The angels give glory to God (Rev. 4:9). And God alone.

At the same time, we may be conscious that when we please God on this earth, we are popular in heaven! The conscious approval of God is one of the most priceless possessions one can have on this planet. One definition of the anointing of the Holy Spirit is the conscious approval of God.

The Sainted Dead

The writer of Hebrews states that when we come to God we come to "the city of the living God, the heavenly Jerusalem. You have come to thousands upon thousands of angels in joyful assembly, to the church of the firstborn, whose names are written in heaven. You have come to God, the Judge of all, to the *spirits of the righteous made perfect*" (Heb. 12:22–23, emphasis added). This is why I said above that there are two categories of beings in heaven apart from the triune God—the angels and the sainted dead. The sainted dead are described as:

1. Righteous
2. Spirits who were
3. Made perfect

They are called "spirits" because they do not have fleshly bodies as we have on the earth. When Paul told of the possibility of being "with Christ" (Phil. 1:23), or "at home with the Lord" (2 Cor. 5:8), he pointed out that to be with Christ in heaven means being "away from the body" (2 Cor. 5:8). And yet earlier in the same chapter he spoke of having an "eternal house in heaven" (v. 1). You could call this a spiritual body. This is why the writer of Hebrews refers to "righteous spirits." Those people in heaven are "spirits." But they are righteous spirits "made perfect." This means that they had a foretaste of glorification. They are in some sense glorified the moment they die; they are therefore called "righteous" and "made perfect." This means they are incapable of being tempted, incapable of being in pain, and incapable of sinning. That said, ultimate glorification comes when Jesus returns, when all bodies will be raised. We will be given glorified bodies. Those in the grave are said to "sleep." This does not mean they are unconscious. "Sleep" is a euphemism to show that the body sleeps. But Paul said that on the day of the final resurrection of the dead all bodies will be raised and "changed" (1 Cor. 15:51). At the second coming of Jesus the bodies of the saved will be glorified and reunited with their spirits, which have been in heaven. This refers to Christians who died: those not alive when Jesus comes again. The sainted dead—righteous spirits made perfect—have been in heaven since they died. As for those who will not see death but be alive when Jesus comes, they will be "caught up" with those who had been in heaven (1 Thess. 4:17).

This chapter has been a bit technical, and a whole book could more easily explain these truths. But the point is this. Those people in heaven at the moment are called "righteous spirits." This would refer to those described in Hebrews 11—all of them: Abel, Enoch, Noah, Abraham, Isaac, Jacob, Joseph, Moses. And *all* those described in Hebrews 11. The disciples of Jesus are there and are among the righteous spirits. All of the original Twelve except for Judas—who was lost (John 17:12)—will be there. Judas sought popularity on earth—and lost it all (Matt. 26:14–16; 27:3–5). Judas is not in heaven. But the other eleven are there. Paul is there. The early Christian martyrs are there. The Saint Augustines and Athanasiuses of this world are there. All those who ever lived whose sins were washed in the blood of Christ are in heaven right now. My mother is there; my father is there. It is my fond hope that I will be there myself in God's time.

Furthermore, the writer of Hebrews was referring to the sainted dead when he said, having finished the previously mentioned Hebrews 11: "Therefore, since we are surrounded by such a great cloud of witnesses, let us throw off everything that hinders and the sin that so easily entangles. And let us run with perseverance the race marked out for us" (Heb. 12:1). He is referring to those in Hebrews 11 who are now described as a "great cloud of witnesses." They not only are on the other side—in glory; they are in some sense looking down at us! To know to what extent the sainted dead in heaven are fully aware of all that is going on here below is unprofitable speculation. But the writer of Hebrews is certainly encouraging us to believe that those described in Hebrews 11 are not only in heaven; they are now "spirits...made perfect" (Heb. 12:23).

This would mean that those in heaven rejoice with those who

are pleasing God on earth! We are popular with the triune God—Father, Son, and Holy Spirit. We are popular with the angels. We are popular with the sainted dead. They are on our side, rooting for us not to give up and to win the race set before us.

So you have a choice—to be popular on earth or be popular in heaven. Which will it be? I hope you choose to be popular in heaven. That is where popularity matters.

Chapter 3

DISAPPOINTED—BUT STILL BELIEVING

These were all commended for their faith, yet none of them received what had been promised.

—Hebrews 11:39

Does God always answer our prayers? Jesus said, "Ask and it will be given to you; seek and you will find; knock and the door will be opened to you. For everyone who asks receives; the one who seeks finds; and to the one who knocks, the door will be opened" (Matt. 7:7–8). He even promised, "You may ask me for anything in my name, and I will do it" (John 14:14). Jesus also gave a parable that had as its purpose that we should keep on praying and never give up (Luke 18:1–8).

The reason we should keep praying and never give up is because God does not always answer our prayers immediately. What is more, we get to know God and His ways by spending more time with Him. One reason I believe God does not answer our prayers immediately is because He likes our company; if He answered all requests straightaway we may not pray as much! But the implication in Jesus' parable is that if we don't give up, God will eventually come to our rescue.

There are those who say, "God has not answered my prayer at all." To which I would respond: *So far as you can tell at the moment.* I myself can testify: there are literally a dozen or more requests I have put to the throne of grace that have not been answered. There are also promises given to me—I believe from the Lord—that have not been fulfilled. And I am eighty-two as I write these lines.

But what about the Enochs, Noahs, Abrahams, Isaacs, and Jacobs of this world? All of those stalwarts in Hebrews 11—heaven's hall of fame—could testify that it was not merely unanswered prayer in their situation; it was a case of God *apparently* not even keeping all His promises! Think about this verse—quoted above: "None of them received what had been promised" (Heb. 11:39). Think about that verse for a moment. *None of them received what had been promised.* Yet they kept believing. But why? Were they dumb? Stupid? Whyever didn't they give up?

It must be said at this stage we do not know *all* that was promised to each of them. We know vaguely and generally what was promised to some of them. But we don't know everything. Based upon Hebrews 11:39, I would conclude that there were things promised to them that are not mentioned in the Old Testament books—as in Genesis, Exodus, Judges, 1 and 2 Samuel, and 1 and 2 Kings for example. If we knew everything that had been promised to them, Hebrews 11:39 would make even more sense. But as this verse stands, we may safely conclude that all those described in Hebrews 11 had the following in common:

1. They did not receive everything that was promised to them.
2. What was promised to them was not so much for them after all, but "for us" so that "together with

us" the promises they received would be perfected or fulfilled.

We might immediately think of Abraham, who was looking for a "city with foundations, whose architect and builder is God" (Heb. 11:10). He did not see that city. We have not seen it either! But it is the New Jerusalem, which together we may all look forward to (Rev. 21 and 22)!

Enoch: A Man Who Pleased God

What was Enoch promised? We know two things for sure: he pleased God and was translated to heaven without dying (Heb. 11:5). What all had he been promised? There is no way to know. Something kept him going. He apparently wrote a book. The book was a prophecy. It referred to the godless men of whom Jude wrote in his brief epistle. Jude quotes Enoch: "See, the Lord is coming with thousands upon thousands of his holy ones to judge everyone, and to convict all of them of all the ungodly acts they have committed in their ungodliness, and of all the defiant words ungodly sinners have spoken against him" (Jude 14–15).

Was Enoch promised that he himself would see the coming of the Lord in his own day? Or did he *think* God promised him this? Who knows? We know from Moses that Enoch "walked faithfully with God; then he was no more, because God took him away" (Gen. 5:24).

My departed friend Dr. Michael Eaton used to say that sometimes God gives a substitute of what we prayed for or what He apparently promised to us—a substitute that is equal or greater than what we actually hoped for. For example, God did not answer Paul's thrice prayed prayer that his thorn in the flesh would be removed, but He promised Paul a greater anointing instead (2 Cor. 12:9). Jesus did not reply to the request of Mary and Martha that He would come to Bethany and heal their brother Lazarus. But

He showed up four days after the funeral and raised Lazarus from the dead—a far better answer to prayer than what Mary and Martha had in mind (John 11:1–44)! Abraham was promised the land of Canaan for an inheritance but was given "no inheritance here, not even enough ground to set his foot on" (Acts 7:5). But his seed inherited the land, if not the whole world (Rom. 4:13)!

The writer of Hebrews says that Enoch was taken to heaven "so that he did not experience death" (Heb. 11:5). Everyone else must die. But God did something unique with Enoch. He loves to treat each of His children in a unique way. Not one single person described in Hebrews 11 had the ease of repeating what had been done before, unless it was Elijah who was taken to heaven without dying—like Enoch. Only Noah built an ark. Only Abraham was commanded to sacrifice his son. Each person in Hebrews had to keep their eyes on God and take instructions from Him. Partly what makes faith *faith* is that you cannot find a precedent to lean on for comfort.

And according to Jude, Enoch was a prophet. Therefore if Enoch did not receive what was promised, could it mean that he himself did not get to see the coming of the Lord with "thousands upon thousands of his holy ones" to convict the men Jude spoke of? In other words, that he did not see the fulfillment of what he prophesied? God could have let Enoch die, but chose to take him away so that he did not experience death. Such a translation to heaven was better than seeing his prophecy fulfilled in his lifetime!

Since Hebrews 11 is, in essence, a list of people who were popular in heaven, let's take a closer look at some of them and see what we can learn.

Abraham: A Man Who Might Have Given Up

As for Abraham, who was promised the land of Canaan for an inheritance but received not even a foot of ground, he is a clear example of not receiving what was promised. In his commentary on Acts 7, John Calvin (1509–1564) observed that Abraham must have felt deceived.[1] But Abraham kept on going. Abraham did not in his lifetime see the literal fulfillment of his seed being as numerable as the stars of the heavens or the sand of the sea. But when God swore an oath to him, it was good as done (Gen. 22:16–18)!

Martin Luther (1483–1546) taught that we must know God as an enemy before we can know Him as a friend. It is like our notion of breaking the betrayal barrier. In the twentieth century aeronautical science broke the sound barrier when a plane could fly faster than the speed of sound. That was an amazing feat. But you and I can beat that! And we don't need to have a PhD in science to achieve it; it is breaking the betrayal barrier! It comes not by education or a high IQ but by persistent faith!

Breaking the betrayal barrier may be experienced by any of us. It is an opportunity to get to know God in an extraordinary way. So many miss this chance. Breaking the betrayal barrier is offered to the believer who suddenly hits a wall. And feels utterly deserted by God. Until that moment he or she was on a roll: a great sense of God, answered prayer, the wind at your back, good health, energy, clear thinking, financial security, everyone affirming you, no problems. Then BAM! No sense of God, friends turn their back on you, financial reverse, ominous medical report, horrible pain. Where is God? Nowhere, it seems.

Many, sadly, give up when that happens. They do not realize that it was a personal invitation from God to get to know Him more intimately and powerfully than ever before.

How many in a spiritual moment—or a religious high—say, "Lord, I love You. I give my life to You. I will never desert You"? Such people often don't realize that God was listening. He replies by saying, "Really?" Then He tests you by giving you a sense of betrayal. As Isaiah put it, "Truly you are a God who has been hiding himself, the God and Savior of Israel" (Isa. 45:15). The psalmist experienced the hiding of God's face from time to time (Ps. 10:11; 13:1–2; 89:46).

When we hit a wall—and feel betrayed—God is treating us with highest dignity. It is an invitation to enter the Big League—with those described in Hebrews 11.

I used to want to be like those described in Hebrews 11. It is an ambition I have had for forty years. I used to challenge the people of Westminster Chapel, "Why can't we all be like those in Hebrews 11?"

I still want it.

So many of us misinterpret bad circumstances and hastily conclude there must be no God. Especially if one is taught that God is only there to make us feel good all the time—prospering us, healing us, and answering all our prayers. Many leaders in the Charismatic movement rejected my book *The Thorn in the Flesh*. Why? Because they taught that such a thorn can be avoided. One of them actually said, "If the apostle Paul had had *my* faith, he wouldn't have had a thorn in the flesh." Amazing that a Christian leader can think like that!

I can never forget the testimony of the ninety-year-old saint of God in Springfield, Illinois, who said, "I have served the Lord for so long that I can hardly tell the difference between a blessing and a trial."

Do you know what it is like to feel betrayed by God? The angels have a word for you: *Congratulations!*

It is an invitation to be popular in heaven.

Isaac: Betrayed but Sticking to His Guns

Isaac, son of Abraham, was one of the most lackluster figures of the Old Testament. And yet he is given a place in Hebrews 11: "By faith Isaac blessed Jacob and Esau in regard to their future" (v. 20). His wife, Rebekah, was barren for many years, but one day God heard Isaac's prayer and she became pregnant. She asked the Lord why the babies in her womb "jostled each other" (Gen. 25:22). The Lord told her:

> Two nations are in your womb,
> and two peoples from within you will be separated;
> one people will be stronger than the other,
> and the older will serve the younger.
>
> —Genesis 25:23

This meant that Esau, who came out of the womb first (v. 25), would give way to Jacob—a reversal of the ancient custom in Israel when the firstborn normally gets double the inheritance.

This also became one of Paul's illustrations to support his teaching on election and predestination. Just before he quoted God's words to Moses, "I will have mercy on whom I will have mercy" (Rom. 9:15; Exod. 33:19), Paul said:

> Before the twins were born or had done anything good or bad—in order that God's purpose in election might stand...she was told, "The older will serve the younger." Just as it is written: "Jacob I loved, but Esau I hated."
>
> —Romans 9:11–13

Toward the end of Isaac's life, when he was going to give his patriarchal blessing to Esau, Jacob betrayed his father and successfully convinced him that he was Esau (Gen. 27:21–29). Esau, being the firstborn, would have received this important blessing. But Jacob tricked his father. Thinking he was blessing Esau, Isaac blessed Jacob. When Isaac realized he had been betrayed, he did not take back what he prophesied concerning Jacob. Said Isaac:

> I blessed him [Jacob]—and indeed he will be blessed!
>
> —Genesis 27:33

Sticking to his guns—having given the blessing to Jacob, Isaac was affirmed by the writer of Hebrews, namely, what he did was "by faith" (Heb. 11:20). In other words, rather than withdraw his blessing and transfer it to Esau, Isaac submitted to the way things turned out, believing that God was behind it all. To put it another way, he put God first, not his firstborn.

Joseph: God Meant It for Good

Joseph the favorite son of Jacob felt this way. He had been given dreams that his eleven brothers would bow down to him. Knowing, as he did, that they hated him and were jealous of him, he looked forward to the day they would affirm him. But instead they sold him to the Ishmaelites, who in turn sold young Joseph to Potiphar, an Egyptian officer in Egypt. While working for Potiphar, Potiphar's own wife began to flirt with Joseph. Here is Joseph in Egypt—a place in which nobody knew him. He had the chance of the "perfect affair": nobody in Egypt knew him, the family back in Canaan would never find out, and Mrs. Potiphar was not going to tell her husband! Having felt let down by God, Joseph might have concluded: "I don't deserve this. God promised me a future of vindication. Here I am stuck in a foreign country. And I deserve some sexual gratification."

But no. He resisted Mrs. Potiphar's flirtation day after day. He may have felt nothing. But the angels said yes! It also meant that God's plans for Joseph—to be prime minister of Egypt one day—would not be aborted.

Billy Graham (1918–2018) once said that it seems the devil gets 75 percent of God's best servants through sexual temptation. Joseph resisted it. So must you. Sooner or later every Christian faces sexual temptation. I will pause and say right now—if *you* are in an affair or are contemplating it, I have this to say: *Stop it!* Stop it now. It is only a matter of time until you would give a thousand worlds to turn the clock back to this very moment.

And yet the thanks Joseph got for doing the right thing is that Mrs. Potiphar falsely accused him of trying to rape her, and he was put in prison (Gen. 39:11–20). What a reward for doing the right thing! Said Peter: "How is it to your credit if you receive a beating for doing wrong and endure it? But if you suffer for doing good and you endure it, this is commendable before God" (1 Pet. 2:20). Joseph suffered for doing good. The Hebrew slave was now judged as being a criminal. In prison with no apparent hope.

Joseph was unpopular on earth but popular in heaven.

You can be sure that those described in Hebrews 11, of whom the world was not worthy, were popular in heaven.

I would prefer to be popular in heaven than to be popular on earth. Would you?

So have you ever felt betrayed by God? Or if betrayed is too strong a word, have you felt that He deserted you? Hid His face from you? Suddenly let bad things happen to you without any notice?

Jacob: All's Well that Ends Well

Jacob left home because he feared that his brother Esau would get vengeance and kill him. His first night away from home was met with a vision from God. It was the first time that Jacob heard directly from God for himself. He grew up knowing about his legendary grandfather Abraham. He had deceived his father, Isaac. He felt totally unworthy and very, very afraid for his future. But God met with him. He saw a stairway resting on the earth with its top reaching heaven and the angels of God ascending and descending on it. Above it stood the Lord who said:

> I am the Lord, the God of your father Abraham and the God of Isaac. I will give you and your descendants the land on which you are lying. Your descendants will be like the dust of the earth, and you will spread out to the west and

> to the east, to the north and to the south. All peoples on earth will be blessed through you and your offspring. I am with you and will watch over you wherever you go, and I will bring you back to this land. I will not leave you until I have done what I promised you.
>
> —Genesis 28:12–15

What a vision! What a promise! And if that were not enough, consider this: God gave him two wives and twelve sons. God prospered him. Rescued him. Preserved him. After that God spoke to Jacob repeatedly, including the night when Jacob wrestled with God, who changed his name to Israel (Gen. 32:28). God reaffirmed his name (Gen. 35:10). Although there were some heartbreaking situations over these years, Jacob was on a roll.

But one day Jacob suddenly hit a wall. He was to experience the worst moment of his life: his son's richly ornamented robe—famously called "the coat of many colors"—was presented to him by his other sons. It was stained with blood. "It is my son's robe! Some ferocious animal has devoured him. Joseph has surely been torn to pieces" (Gen. 37:33).

The twelve sons are now only eleven. Ishmael, Abraham's son of impatience, had also been promised twelve sons (Gen. 17:20; 25:16). "Surely I too should have twelve sons if these promises of God are true," Jacob must have thought. With only eleven sons and his beloved Joseph out of the picture, the future for Jacob was bleak. All those promises have come to nothing, he may well have thought.

But behind all this God was at work. When the writer of Hebrews chose one moment of Jacob's life to mention when writing the illustrious chapter on the people of faith, the writer chose to say this: "By faith Jacob, when he was dying, blessed each of Joseph's sons, and worshipped as he leaned on the top of his staff" (Heb. 11:21). What gratitude Jacob must have felt.

God was at the bottom of it all. And yes, God meant it for good (Gen. 50:10). For further details, see my books *All's Well That Ends Well*[2] and *God Meant It for Good*.[3]

Every sovereign vessel must break the betrayal barrier. A sovereign vessel is a man or woman raised up by God for an unusual purpose. I believe that many believers at some point in their lives receive an invitation from God to be a sovereign vessel. But not all accept that invitation. That invitation comes through a feeling of being severely let down by God. It is how you *respond* to that feeling that will determine whether you become a sovereign vessel.

Have you hit a wall? Congratulations! Does it feel like all hell has broken loose and God Himself has left you?

I answer my question for you and offer this counsel: take hold of the adverse situation you are in with both hands! Accept it. Affirm it. See it as a gift from God. Or, as the hymn "Like a River Glorious" put it:

> Every joy or trial falleth from above,
> Traced upon our dial by the Sun of love;
> We may trust Him fully, all for us to do;
> They who trust Him wholly find Him wholly true.
>
> —Frances R. Havergal (1836–1879)

Moses: He Wanted the Reward

Moses broke the betrayal barrier. There were two phases of Moses' life. The first was when he was forty years old, living in luxury in Pharaoh's palace, and he decided to visit his fellow Israelites. Stephen said, "It came into his *heart* to visit his brothers, the children of Israel" (Acts 7:23, esv, emphasis added). Did *God* put this desire in his heart? Yes. Moses grew up knowing he was circumcised. He knew he was different from other Egyptian boys. He knew for many years that those Israelites—suffering under the ruthless leadership of the Pharaoh—were his *brothers*. He could have dismissed this as "bad luck for them, good luck for me." But that was not Moses. He had a conscience. He was a sovereign vessel. He also knew in his heart of hearts that the God of the Israelites was *his God.* There was a huge purpose in all this. He could take it no more; he decided to show the Israelites that he was on their side. To do this he killed an Egyptian. Moses thought this would send a signal to all the Israelites that he was one of them and was determined to deliver them.

But everything backfired. He thought that surely his own people would realize that God was using him to rescue them, but they didn't. Moses sought to intervene in a fight between two Israelites. He said to them, "Men, you are brothers; why do you wrong each other?" The reply: "Who made you a ruler and judge over us? Do you want to kill me as you killed the Egyptian yesterday?" (vv. 26–28).

This was the moment that God appeared to betray Moses. He had nailed his colors to the mast—and was utterly rejected by his brothers. He was in a no-win situation; rejected by the Israelites and unwelcome back in the palace of Pharaoh. He had unwittingly reached the point of no return.

What kept him going? We would not know exactly what it was were it not for what the writer of Hebrews says: "He was looking ahead to the reward" (Heb. 11:26). Yes, he counted disgrace for the sake of Christ as having greater value than the treasures of Egypt. But Moses knew that the reward down the road was greater!

Why suffer being betrayed? Because if we break through the betrayal barrier we will be so glad we did! Simple as that. The reward is worth it.

By the way, don't be intimidated or put off by the notion of reward—as if this is beneath you! God has *always* appealed to our own interest to get our attention! Do not think you are a cut above most people who lower themselves by wanting a reward! If you think like that, you are being self-righteous, if not silly.

Moses did not give up. What is more, God did not truly use him for another forty years! It was when he was eighty that God began to use Moses. Dr. Martyn Lloyd-Jones used to say to me, "The worst thing that can happen to a man is to succeed before he was ready." Moses was not ready when he was forty. But at eighty? Yes.

We come to the second phase of Moses' life. He soon learned the pain of leadership from on-the-job training that his followers—the Israelites—would be vacillating in their respect and obedience to him. In one moment they were carrying Moses on their shoulders. But when the Pharaoh required the Israelites to find their own straw to make bricks—and did not reduce the quota—they turned on Moses. "May the Lord look on you and judge you! You have made us obnoxious to Pharaoh and his officials and have put a sword in their hand to kill us" (Exod. 5:20–21). Moses then poured out his heart to God: "Why, Lord, why have you brought trouble on this people?... You have not rescued your people at all" (vv. 22–23), having been promised that God would rescue them.

But after Moses comes toward the end of his life, we see him with yet a different but most intense desire. Having been assured that he pleased the Lord, Moses put this request: "If you are pleased with me, *teach me your ways so I may know you* and continue to find favor with you" (Exod. 33:13, emphasis added).

I am unable to describe adequately what that verse has meant to me. Having read it a thousand times, one day I read it as if for the first time. I was so convicted. I felt so ashamed. I asked myself: "If I knew I pleased the Lord and could then ask for anything I wanted from Him, would I have put a request like Moses'?"

It made me see what the real Moses was like. It made me see what I am like. I fear I would have asked for something selfish. Perhaps a greater anointing. Moses wanted to know God's *ways*. It reminds me of Paul in his older, more mature years: "I want to know Christ—yes to know the power of his resurrection and the participation in his sufferings, becoming like him in his death" (Phil. 3:10).

Popular in heaven. Moses' determination to break through the betrayal barrier because of the reward coming later was an ambition that was popular in heaven. God did reward him. He became the greatest leader of men in human history. His devotion to God and accomplishments for Him became so great that the whole of the Old Testament could be summed up in one name: Moses. The whole of the New Testament could be summed up in one name: Jesus Christ. "For the law was given through Moses; grace and truth came through Jesus Christ" (John 1:17).

Joshua: Put in His Place

God promised Joshua, "As I was with Moses, so I will be with you; I will never leave you nor forsake you" (Josh. 1:5). I cannot imagine more comforting words than that. Imagine the task of succeeding Moses. Talk about being intimidated! But such a promise from the God of Moses was sweet to Joshua—but also scary. Joshua was given the task to go with specific instructions, "since you have never been this way before" (Josh. 3:4).

Just before the children of Israel crossed over the Jordan River, Joshua saw a man standing in front of him with a drawn sword. Joshua went up to him and asked, "Are you for us or for our enemies?" Then came the surprising reply: "Neither...but as commander of the army of the Lord I have now come" (Josh. 5:13–14). This was an angel.

What is going on here? Surely God is on Israel's side! The angel's comment smacks all over of being a betrayal! But it was for Israel generally and Joshua particularly. And for all of us. God does things for His own glory. Once we have gotten to know the Lord a bit, there is a tendency in all of us to begin to take ourselves too seriously. I have this problem. What God was doing for

Joshua was this: putting Joshua in his place and keeping him from getting a feeling of entitlement.

Those who have been right in the middle of the Lord's work often find themselves feeling they deserve special privileges, especially if they have sacrificed a lot. Take those who have become missionaries in foreign countries. Or anyone who has sacrificed much in personal privileges for the kingdom of God. Jesus dealt with this in one of His parables: "So you also, when you have done everything you were told to do, should say, 'We are unworthy servants; we have only done our duty'" (Luke 17:10). That word has put me in my place more than once.

Joshua succeeded Moses therefore in that he too was required to take off his shoes (Josh. 5:15). Moses was required to worship barefooted when he was commanded not to come too close to the burning bush. And now the same thing is put on Joshua: he too must take off his sandals lest he begin to think he has some sort of a "claim" on God. My old mentor Dr. N. B. Magruder once wrote me a note that I carried for years: "The only evidence that I have seen the Divine Glory is my willingness to forsake any claim upon God." That word continues to stagger me. It reminds me of the lyrics of the hymn "When I Survey the Wondrous Cross":

> Love so amazing, so divine,
> Demands my soul, my life, my all.
>
> —Isaac Watts (1674–1748)

Samuel: A Man Who Learned Not to Take Himself so Seriously

Samuel was the first of a new era of prophets in the Old Testament. He appeared on the scene in a day when the word of God was "rare" (1 Sam. 3:1). There were some people with prophetic gifts between the times of Moses and Samuel. Deborah, for example, who might have been mentioned rather than Barak in Hebrews

11:32 (see Judges 4 and 5). But most are not explicitly mentioned; hence the comment about the word of God being "rare"—meaning not many visions, not many prophetic words. But God raised up Samuel, an answer to his mother's prayers (1 Sam. 1:27).

It was Samuel who warned Israel not to have a king. He pleaded with them. He knew they were making a grave, fatal mistake (1 Sam. 8:10–20). But God said to Samuel, "Listen to them and give them a king" (v. 22). If Samuel were like some of us, he would have said, "God, I told them they should not have a king. Don't let me lose face like this. I must stick to my guns and tell them they are not to have a king." But no. Samuel took God's word with dignity *and*... did all he could to find the best man in Israel. He found Saul and affirmed him to the hilt.

Samuel was right in two ways:

1. Israel was indeed making a horrible mistake.
2. He obeyed God and did not argue back.

But there is more. After accepting the verdict that Saul was now rejected by God (1 Sam. 16:1), Samuel now shows a willingness to go outside his comfort zone and look for a new king—even while there was a king alive and well!

Samuel was already a legend. One might suppose that God would say to Samuel, "Samuel, you have served Me well. I am going to let you retire and spend the rest of your days relaxing on a beach near the ocean." But no. "Go to the house of Jesse," to find the next king. It was a dangerous mission.

Is this relevant for you? Do you feel you have served God well up to now and that it is now time for a long holiday without having to work more or risk your reputation again?

Perhaps you are like Samuel. You have more work to do for God—and it won't be easy!

And yet we are to find one more amazing thing about Samuel.

He jumps the gun when he comes to the house of Jesse and assumes that Eliab will be the next king. He made his feelings known to Jesse. He looked at Eliab, and said, "Surely the Lord's anointed stands here before the Lord" (1 Sam. 16:6). But Samuel got it wrong. God then said to him, "Do not consider his appearance or his height, for I have rejected him. The Lord does not look at the things people look at. People look at the outward appearance, but the Lord looks at the heart" (v. 7).

Samuel had to make a choice: either to stick to his guns and say, "Eliab is the next king," or to say humbly, "I made a mistake, Jesse; sorry. The next king will not be your firstborn, Eliab." He climbed down before all.

I am afraid there are prophetic people—and some not so prophetic—who, if they have taken a stand or theological position, will not admit they got it wrong. For example, if they wrote it in a book but later found out they were wrong, they won't admit it. Shame. Or if they gave a prophetic announcement and later found out they were wrong, they won't apologize and admit they were wrong. Shame.

Samuel was not concerned about his prophetic reputation. He was more concerned to be popular in heaven. Samuel had a careful look at each of Jesse's sons but had to say that the Lord's anointed was not among them. Only by insisting that Jesse call for young David—the last person anybody would have picked—was Samuel allowed to say, "This is the one" (v. 12).

Had Samuel been like so many of us who take ourselves so seriously, he would have argued back with God regarding Israel and a king—about having to risk his life further by pursuing the next king while Saul was still alive, and about having to back down when he had made it clear he thought that Eliab was the next king.

But Samuel did not take himself seriously. That is the reason

God could use him. Being popular with God and the angels meant more to Samuel than saving face before people.

David: A Man After God's Own Heart

Whereas some of the feats of those people of faith in Hebrews 11 are spelled out somewhat, others are not; only their names are mentioned, Gideon, Barak, Samson, Jephthah, David, Samuel, "and the prophets" (v. 32). It is easy to overlook "and the prophets"—which would include the noncanonical prophets (such as Elijah and Elisha) and canonical prophets (such as Isaiah, Jeremiah, Ezekiel, Daniel, and others). Other exploits are described without their names being mentioned. May I urge you please to read the next lines carefully:

> Who through faith conquered kingdoms, administered justice, and gained what was promised; who shut the mouths of lions, quenched the fury of the flames, and escaped the edge of the sword; whose weakness was turned to strength; and who became powerful in battle and routed foreign armies. Women received back their dead, raised to life again. There were others who were tortured, refusing to be released so that they might gain an even better resurrection. Some faced jeers and flogging, and even chains and imprisonment. They were put to death by stoning; they were sawed in two; they were killed by the sword. They went about in sheepskins and goatskins, destitute, persecuted and mistreated—the world was not worthy of them. They wandered in deserts and mountains, living in caves and in holes in the ground. These were all commended for their faith, yet none of them received what had been promised.
>
> —Hebrews 11:33–39

You might detect an apparent contradiction above: some "gained what was promised" and "yet none of them received what was promised." This means that some of them were enabled to see their prayers answered in their lifetime; but *all* of them had to wait for the major thing that kept them going! For example, David lived to see the prophecy of Samuel regarding David being king fulfilled in his lifetime. Yes. But David did *not* see the fulfillment of the promised Messiah in his own day: "The LORD says to my lord: 'Sit at my right hand until I make your enemies a footstool for your feet.'" (Ps. 110:1). He did not see the true fulfillment of Psalm 16, which refers to the resurrection of Jesus Christ and His being clearly revealed by the coming of the Spirit at Pentecost:

> I have set the LORD always before me;
> Because He is at my right hand I shall not be moved.
> Therefore my heart is glad, and my glory rejoices;
> My flesh also will rest in hope.
> For You will not leave my soul in Sheol,
> Nor will You allow Your Holy One to see corruption.
> You will show me the path of life;
> In Your presence is fullness of joy;
> At Your right hand are pleasures forevermore.
>
> —PSALM 16:8–11, NKJV; SEE ALSO ACTS 2:25–35

In some cases it is easy to figure out who these people are in Hebrews 11:33–39, but not in all cases. It is easy to see the three Hebrew children from the Book of Daniel, to see the ministry of Elijah and Elisha. But others were people who will remain unknown to us until we see them in heaven. Though unknown here, these people were popular in heaven. As for David, he was brought into prominence right out of the blue. While his older brothers were each hoping to be chosen by Samuel to be the next king, David was looking after the sheep. He was not even notified that the great Samuel had come to his house for dinner! It did not cross Jesse's mind that his youngest son would be selected by Samuel. Oh how Jesse underestimated teenager David!

Can you identify with David at this point? Do you have an authority figure—parent, pastor, teacher, relative—who did not expect much out of you? Or even said, "You will never amount to anything"? It can be very painful to hear something negative said of you. It can be traumatic and cause a scar on your psyche for the rest of your life. In 1945, when I was ten years old, my teacher in Crabbe Elementary School in Ashland, Kentucky, told my father (I wish I had never heard it), "R. T. is not an A student." Until I was ten, I pretty much made straight As in school. But this teacher for some reason did not like me. I got Bs and Cs from her. Her nephew, who was also in the class, got straight As. Not me. I never became an A student again. I let those words govern me for many years. It would be another twenty-five years—when I enrolled in seminary in 1970—before I actually came into my own.

Samuel took the horn of oil and anointed David in the presence of his brothers, "and from that day on the Spirit of the Lord came powerfully upon David" (1 Sam. 16:13). And yet David was a nobody. King Saul still wore the crown but lost the anointing—that is, the conscious approval of God. Saul had the following; David had no following. Saul became yesterday's man; David was tomorrow's man. Saul had the prestige; David had no prestige. Saul had the "mailing list." Saul was popular on earth. David was without any popularity at that time. His task: to learn what it would take to be popular in heaven.

If only Samuel had said, having anointed David to be king, "Oh by the way, David, I must tell you that it will be another twenty years before you become king. And one more thing, you will spend the next twenty years running from King Saul just to stay alive. This is part of your preparation to be king." But no. David had only one thing: the anointing of the Holy Spirit. He had to learn the rest.

David is referred to twice in the Bible as "a man after God's own heart" (1 Sam. 13:14; Acts 13:22). That would be a most suitable expression for being popular in heaven!

David had a lot to learn at that stage. Some might have thought that having the anointing of the Spirit is sufficient to qualify a man to be king. Wrong. David was far from ready to be king. The worst thing that can happen to a man is to succeed before he is ready. That is precisely what happened to Saul. God was determined that David not succeed until he was ready.

That said, there came a moment when David was unpopular in heaven. It goes to show that a person's popularity in heaven may wane. The same man—the only person in the Bible called a man "after God's own heart"—was involved in what is arguably the most heinous, despicable, and disgraceful sin in all Holy Writ. He lusted after another man's wife, Bathsheba, slept with her, and she became pregnant. In an effort to cover up the sin, he summoned her husband, Uriah, to come home to spend time with his wife. But Uriah's refusal to sleep with her did not go according to David's plan. He then had Uriah killed in the battle (2 Sam. 11). No human being in Scripture sunk lower than that. But David was found out by the prophet Nathan. David was not defensive, but quickly repented (2 Sam. 12). Though severely chastened for his folly, as the second part of David's life demonstrated (2 Sam. 13–15), David was restored (Ps. 51).

Even though God did not let David succeed until he was ready, the man after God's own heart was not perfect. Nor will you be when your time has come.

This aspect of David's life is an encouragement to all. That he would be called a man after God's own heart shows that one does not have to be perfect to be loved by God. It also shows that we can be popular in heaven and then be unpopular for a while. But thank God that need not be the end of the story. Have you fallen? Have you made the angels blush by your folly? Take courage; God is not finished with you yet!

We are all a work under construction, as Ruth Graham (1920–2007) put it. On her tombstone are these words: "End of construction—thank you for your patience."

Are you tomorrow's man? Tomorrow's woman? You may have the anointing. But that in itself does not qualify you. Every person's anointing needs to be refined. Victor Hugo (1802–1885) said, "Like the trampling of a mighty army so is the force of an idea whose time has come." I would rephrase that: like the trampling of a mighty army so is the force of one's *anointing* whose time has come." Over the next twenty years David would learn how to survive in impossible situations, how to discover the sensitivity of the Holy Spirit, the need for wisdom, the importance of the word *mercy*, the need to learn gratitude. David was far from ready to be king on that day when Samuel poured the oil on him. But his time eventually came; it was worth waiting for. He became the greatest king Israel ever had. For further study on the people mentioned in this chapter see my book on Hebrews 11, *Believing God*,[4] as well as my books *The Anointing*[5] and *A Man After God's Own Heart*.[6]

The people described in Hebrews 11 were not popular on earth. Many of them were hated. And they all had to suffer incalculable disappointment along the way. But during the whole time of their preparation and accomplishments—and lack of fulfillment, "none of them received what had been promised"—they were popular in heaven. The whole time. They also had in common that they chose a road less traveled:

> Two roads diverged in a wood, and I—
> I took the one less traveled by,
> And that has made all the difference.[7]
>
> —Robert Frost (1874–1963)

Chapter 4

POPULARITY IN HEAVEN: AN EARTHLY CHOICE

He [Moses] chose to be mistreated along with the people of God rather than to enjoy the fleeting pleasures of sin. He regarded disgrace for the sake of Christ as of greater value than the treasures of Egypt, because he was looking ahead to his reward.

—Hebrews 11:25–26

If it is your heart's desire to be popular in heaven, and I hope it is, I must caution you: God will not knock you down to make it happen! It is going to be true with you only if you make a conscious decision to be popular in heaven. This does not mean that you will be favored over the saints there; it is not like being popular in school when you are good looking or excel in sports. It means that you are a beautiful fragrance that ascends to the place of the saints and the angels; that your choices on planet earth cohere with the holy will of God being carried out in heaven. Right choices on earth fit well with the saints there! It is like the petition in the Lord's Prayer: "Your will be done, on earth as it is in heaven" (Matt. 6:10). In heaven the will of God is being carried out perfectly; there is no rebellion, no rivalry among the saints, or grumbling there. So when we make decisions on earth that fit in with what is pleasing to God, we are not only *praying* that the will of God be done in our lives, but actually *carrying out* His will as it is in heaven. This makes us popular in the heavenlies!

When I preach on total forgiveness—as I have done many times—I make the point: total forgiveness is *a choice*. You must decide to do it. You choose to forgive. God will not overcome you and throw you to the floor to get your attention. You must—out of conviction that it is the right thing to do—consciously, voluntarily, deliberately, and once-for-all make a choice: forgive them. Totally. Let them off the hook. Kiss vengeance goodbye and pray for them to be *blessed*. That's the way it is done.

Moses made a deliberate and once-for-all *choice* to be unpopular on earth. He was looking ahead to his "reward." He knew that his decision would be popular in heaven. He never looked back.

As totally forgiving your enemies goes against nature, so too choosing to be unpopular on earth goes against nature. To put it another way, in the same way that we by nature want to see our enemy punished and exposed, so we by nature want to be popular. That is because of two things:

1. The way God made us before the fall
2. Being the sons and daughters of Adam and Eve, who sinned in the Garden of Eden

We are all created in the image of God. This is manifested in part by the way God wants us to affirm Him—to bless Him, to honor Him, to accept Him as He is. In the same way we all are made to want people to affirm us and to accept us. These things said, the problem is heightened and complicated by our being sinful creatures. We are all sinners; all of us have sinned and come short of the glory of God (Rom. 3:23). We crave the attention and approval of people. By nature we want to be popular.

Do you want to be popular? Of course you do. So do I. If I told you I did not want to be popular on earth you may rightly call me a fraud. There are certain things we never outgrow, no matter how close to God we are. We will always want to be popular. If you deny this, you are almost certainly playing games with yourself, not to mention imputing to yourself a level of godliness and superhuman grace that isn't there. We are not glorified yet! Furthermore, as I said, God made us this way. We want to be accepted; we want to be liked.

Many years ago I read Dale Carnegie's book *How to Win Friends and Influence People.*[1] I also took the course. It helped me immensely as a person, not to mention when I was a door-to-door vacuum cleaner salesman. One of the major points I make in my book *Total Forgiveness* and when I preach on it is that we must let the other person "save face." I got that point from Carnegie's teaching. In other words, instead of rubbing their noses in it, you set them free from feeling guilty! Carnegie uses this to show how to win friends. He teaches that the greatest desire in the world, even stronger than the sexual desire, is the desire to feel important.

Popularity Makes a Person Feel Important

The temptation to be popular on earth rather than be popular in heaven will not go away. Neither you nor I will become so godly that we are not tempted to be popular on earth rather than popular in heaven.

The purpose of this book is not to make you feel guilty because you are tempted to be popular on earth. If you did not care what people think, why comb your hair when you get up? Why brush your teeth? Why get dressed? Not to want to do these things sometimes suggests a degree of mental illness. Not only did God create us with a desire to have significance, we must therefore never forget that we are sinful creatures as a consequence of the fall of Adam and Eve in the Garden of Eden. We are sinners, even after we become Christians. If we say we have no sin, we deceive ourselves and the truth is not in us (1 John 1:8). To quote Martin Luther: the Christian is "simultaneous saint and sinner."[2] No matter how holy we become, we will need to sing these words:

> Prone to wander, Lord I feel it,
> Prone to leave the God I love;
> Here's my heart, O take and seal it,
> Seal it for Thy courts above.
>
> —Robert Robinson (1735–1790)

These things said, as followers of Jesus Christ we want to be more like Him and discover ways in which we please Him. We will never be perfectly like Jesus on this earth. The joy of pursuing an unachievable goal is the Christian's lot. It is what we discover when we seek to be like Jesus: joy and blessing in trying to be more like Him! One of the ways we pursue this goal is to seek not to be popular on earth but in heaven.

We have to make a choice: either choosing to be popular on earth as our priority or popular in heaven. We don't need motivation to be popular on earth! Whereas we may need a lot of help with learning how to win friends and influence people, the *desire* to feel important on earth hardly needs to be taught! We get this from being born.

However, to become popular in heaven we must fight against the natural desire to be important on earth. For some this will be very hard indeed. The degree to which we resist the temptation to become popular on earth as opposed to being popular in heaven will be the degree to which we will be popular in heaven.

But, as I said before, the willingness to become unpopular on earth is to go against nature! Whoever could naturally *choose* to become mistreated with the people of God?

And yet Moses did precisely that. Consider these three things he chose to do (Heb. 11:25–26):

1. To be mistreated with the people of God
2. To resist the pleasures of sin
3. To embrace disgrace for the sake of Christ

When he made the initial decision to visit his brothers, the children of Israel, he was choosing to be among them and be mistreated with them. His brothers in Israel were slaves—having to build the ancient pyramids in Egypt with bricks they made out of straw. It was a horrible way to live. But Moses chose to do that.

The people of God in Moses' day suffered physical pain and suffering—being slaves to make bricks for the pharaoh. It wasn't fun. But the people of God in the day of the writer of Hebrews were Christians—Jews and Gentiles—who suffered many kinds of persecution. Some suffered physically. Some were tortured. But all suffered shame and disgrace. It was *so* unpopular to be a follower of Jesus in those days. We can hardly understand it today—that is, in America.

Moses chose this in his day. The writer calls it "disgrace for the sake of Christ"! You may ask, "How could the writer of Hebrews talk like that? Moses lived thirteen hundred years before Jesus came!" Granted. But there is a common thread in all persecution against the people of God—summarized as hatred, disgust, contempt, and a feeling of no sympathy for such people. The people of God from all ages have this in common: *The world hates God's people. The world hates God. The world hates His Son. The world will hate us.* This thread, in a sense, holds all the people of God together from every generation. I am gripped by these words: "I, John, your brother and companion in the suffering and kingdom and patient endurance that are ours in Jesus" (Rev. 1:9). John is reaching out to all of us who read the Book of Revelation, especially when we have experienced persecution for Jesus' sake.

Moses Made the Choice to Suffer Disgrace and Suffering

But why? There were two factors: first, God had done a work of grace in his heart that made him want to choose it. God does not compel us against our will, but makes us willing to go. Second, Moses rightly calculated in his mind that such a decision would have wonderful consequences—a reward down the road. What is more, staying in the palace of the king of Egypt would be a temporary pleasure. Sweet are the "pleasures of sin for a season" (Heb. 11:25). Only for a while. What God gives as a reward lasts forever. Moses discerned this. "He regarded disgrace for the sake of Christ as of greater value than the treasures of Egypt, because he was looking ahead to his reward" (v. 26).

Imagine this—choosing disgrace! But listen to this: John and Peter were flogged by the order of the Sanhedrin—the ancient Jewish court that governed Israel—made up of priests, Pharisees, and Sadducees. The apostles were beaten. It caused physical pain that brought blood. But did they complain? Absorb this if you will (sometimes I cannot read this without coming to tears): "The apostles left the Sanhedrin, rejoicing because they had been counted worthy of suffering disgrace for the Name" (Acts 5:41). Were they complaining? Were they saying, "How could this happen to us?" "How could God do this?" "What have we done to deserve this?" No. The truth is, they couldn't believe their luck! They were having to pinch themselves that they were "counted worthy of suffering disgrace for the Name." They were saying to themselves, "God is so good to us. We don't deserve to suffer for Jesus. But He has chosen us!"

Amazing, isn't it?

In the same way that Moses looked to his reward, you can be

totally sure that Peter and John knew this was a wonderful earnest of God's goodness to them! Suffering for Jesus isn't for nothing! It is worth everything. It is priceless. "In all this you greatly rejoice," said Peter, "though now for a little while you may have had to suffer grief in all kinds of trials. These have come so that the proven genuineness of your faith—of greater worth than gold, which perishes even though refined by fire—may result in praise, glory and honor when Jesus Christ is revealed" (1 Pet. 1:6–7).

Are you suffering for the Lord Jesus Christ at the moment? Congratulations! This is the way to enter the Big League, as I said. Not only that, it is also an invitation to be a sovereign vessel—the highest calling in the world. Greater than being president, prime minister, or king!

Five Chief Temptations

As we saw previously, there is a difference between temptation and sin. It is not a sin to be tempted; Jesus was tempted (Heb. 4:15). Sin is yielding to temptation. The list of temptations to be resisted is much greater than the five that head this section. But if you and I will deal with these, we will be making great strides to being popular in heaven.

John admonished us not to love the world or "anything in the world" (1 John 2:15; "the *things* that are in the world," KJV, emphasis added). Those "things" to which John refers are probably best summed up in three words: sex, money, pride. For they are implied in the following verse: "The cravings of sinful man, the lust of his eyes and the boasting of what he has and does" (1 John 2:16, NIV 1984). I would understand John's order to be sex—"the cravings of sinful man"; money—"the lust of the eyes"; and pride—"the boasting of what he has and does." And yet the lust of the eyes and the cravings of sinful man are surely interchangeable.

1. Sex

Sex was not born in Hollywood but at the throne of grace, as Dr. Clyde Narramore (1916–2015) used to teach. This is the way God made us. Sexual desire is natural; it is a physical need. But the Bible has nonetheless imposed parameters—guidelines, restrictions—when it comes to sexual gratification. In short, sexual fulfillment is reserved for heterosexual, monogamous marriage. It is not like food or water, which you must have to survive. Though sex is a natural desire, one can survive without sexual fulfillment. Martin Luther is quoted as saying that God uses sex to drive a man to marriage, ambition to drive a man to service, and fear to drive a man to faith. There are three Greek words that are translated "love" into English: *eros* (physical or sexual love), *philia* (brotherly love), *agape* (unselfish love). The big lie that needs to be exposed is that the *eros* love that makes a man and woman want to get married is sufficient to sustain the marriage. In order for a marriage to survive, *agape* love must parallel (not replace) sexual love.

These things said, sexual desire and sexual temptation have been with all of us from an early age. Sex is on most people's minds in varying degrees. Always has been, always will be. It is what led to David's downfall (2 Sam. 11), and his son Amnon's downfall (2 Sam. 13). Sadly, currently hundreds of church leaders fall every year from not resisting sexual temptation. Adultery is the predominant moving force of Hollywood, the leading factor behind most best-selling books, the thread that usually holds TV shows together, and a real motivation in the world that has become more and more anti-God.

Let me share something rather ironic. I just turned on the TV after finishing the above paragraph. The news announced: "*Playboy* founder Hugh Hefner dies at the age of ninety-one." I immediately asked: "Where is this man right now?" He popularized almost every kind of sexual attraction imaginable, glorified sex outside of marriage, and flagrantly extolled the act of adultery. He had three wives and many sexual partners and did more than any other person to change the perception of morality in America. He possibly had more sexual activity than any human being in our lifetime. He treated women—he called them "bunnies"—like things, and these bunnies seemed to go along with it. What was considered disgusting and reprehensible in 1953 (when *Playboy* began with Marilyn Monroe on the cover) became tolerated in the next generation; the early issues of *Playboy* look tame compared to what developed over the years. *Playboy* became so acceptable that even a candidate for president was interviewed in *Playboy.*

Hugh Hefner made a decision to be popular on earth. He succeeded. Oh yes. And yet I cannot help but wonder what Hugh Hefner is thinking right now—as I write these lines. I can tell you this much: he is conscious in Hades (Gr. grave) and has to spend eternity knowing the way he chose to live his life.

Rejected—accepted—popular

Sometimes relationships go through stages—from lyrical, to disillusionment, and to reality. When it comes to morality, you often have a progression: what is initially horrible becomes acceptable and eventually popular. Take the way public viewpoint has shifted on the matter of marriage. Heterosexual marriage for life with one partner was an assumption for thousands of years. Then came the destigmatizing of homosexual relationships. Gay marriage was initially regarded by the majority of people as being detestable. That was barely over ten years ago (as I write these lines).

Think about how quickly much of the world has changed on this matter! When Barack Obama first ran for president in 2008, he was against homosexual marriage, but he endorsed it during his second term. Hence the downward progression from rejection to acceptance to popularity. Today we have a jaded generation;

pornography is everywhere. Infidelity is common. Virginity is laughed at. Few couples enter marriage today without having slept together. And many heterosexual couples don't even get married. We live in the "me generation," which reminds us of the Book of Judges: everyone did what seemed fit in their own eyes (Judg. 21:25).

Sexual promiscuity is what often lies behind the world wanting to believe in evolution. Sir Julian Huxley (1887–1975), one of the world's leading defendants of Darwinian evolution, admitted that the world jumped to believe in evolution because of sex. Interviewed on the *Merv Griffin Show* in 1969 Huxley was asked: "Why was Darwin and evolution so quickly accepted without any proof?" He replied: "I suppose it was the idea of God interfering with our sexual mores."[3] Therefore the more some scientists were seen to support evolution, the more rampant sexual promiscuity became.

Sexual promiscuity is largely what lies behind the world accepting same-sex marriage. If creation according to Genesis 1 and 2 is true, that means that God created us; that humankind is male and female (Gen. 1:27). That is the foundation for the biblical view of marriage as further indicated by Genesis 2:24: "That is why a man leaves his father and mother and is united to his wife, and they will become one flesh." But if evolution is true, the Bible is apparently false. That said, I am very aware of many Christians who accept theistic evolution. That number is increasing every day. And yet the idea of evolution would not have been thought of had not Darwin said it first.

According to John, "the cravings of sinful man" is one of the things that must be brought under control. I put sex at the top of the list, although some might put money or pride first.

2. Money

> For the love of money is a root of all kinds of evil. Some people, eager for money, have wandered from the faith and pierced themselves with many griefs.
>
> —1 Timothy 6:10

I have seen it happen again and again. I have watched friends vainly imagine that making big money would bring happiness. I have watched marriages break down, homes divide, and children suffer because one thought that making money would bring happiness. And, yes, it can do that—to some degree. This is why it is written that "money is the answer for everything" (Eccles. 10:19). But the writer of these words is not stating an absolute principle: money will not buy true joy, wisdom, inner peace, a happy marriage, or get you to heaven. And yet he states a practical reality; money provides a measure of security—for food, shelter, and clothing. Relief. Having some money is better than having nothing when it comes to survival. We cannot exist without the essentials of food, clothing, and shelter.

A case can be made that Jesus had more to say about money than any other subject. Take the following statements He made in the Sermon on the Mount. "Do not store up for yourselves treasures on earth, where moth and vermin destroy, and where thieves beak in and steal. But store up for yourselves treasures in heaven, where moth and vermin do not destroy, and where thieves do not break in and steal. For where your treasure is, there your heart will be also" (Matt. 6:19–21). He went on to say, "No one can serve two masters. Either you will hate the one and love the other, or you will be devoted to the one and despise the other. You cannot serve God and money" (v. 24).

The most comforting truth of all, moreover, is that God—our Father—takes the responsibility for feeding and clothing us. He does! For this reason Jesus tells us not to worry. We should not worry about life, what we will eat or drink, or what we will wear. If our heavenly Father feeds birds, how much more valuable are we than they? "So do not worry, saying, 'What shall we eat?' or 'What shall we drink?' or 'What shall we wear?'" After all, "your heavenly Father knows" that we need these things (Matt. 6:25–32). Then comes what is almost certainly the most important verse in the Bible when it comes to money. It was my dad's favorite verse; he must have quoted it a thousand times: "Seek first his kingdom and his righteousness, and all these things will be given to you as well" (v. 33).

I would say that Matthew 6:33 is not only the most important verse in the Bible about money; it is also the most neglected. Here is why: Matthew 6:33 deals with what is essential to us—food, shelter, and clothing. God Himself takes the responsibility for these things. But our problem is *greed*. We want more. And that is where the love of money moves into our lives, and the consequence is loss of peace and joy, and the oncoming of anxiety, trouble, heartbreak, and grief—just as Paul warned (1 Tim. 6:10).

What is even more troubling is the way some Christian preachers treat Matthew 6:33 with contempt and tempt sincere people with prosperity and wealth when that is *not* what Jesus is talking about in the Sermon on the Mount. It is a pity that Christian leaders dangle the hope of luxuries before people's eyes when Jesus never promised these things. It is true that some of God's choice servants have been wealthy—such as Abraham. But not all sovereign vessels are promised to be like Abraham in every way. "Godliness with contentment is great gain" (1 Tim. 6:6). This is what will make you popular in heaven.

I will never forget the look on the face of a woman in my old church in Ashland, Kentucky. She was very spiritual, very godly, and very poor. Her husband did not seem to care for her. He had a job that did not pay well. And yet this woman had a look of brightness—a shine on her face. She was the type you brought your prayer requests to. She carried a sense of the presence of God. I remember her so well. But I also remember the look on her face after her husband died suddenly. He had an insurance policy that left her very well off financially. All were pleased for her. But the shine on her face diminished, the tears of joy from the presence of God dried up. I found it so sad. It is what money does to so many people.

The wonderful thing is, God takes the responsibility for feeding us, clothing us, and giving us a place to live. What He wants of us is to believe this. And trust Him. And fight off any feeling of jealousy toward those who seem to have so much more than we do. The psalmist recounts how his feet had "almost slipped" because he foolishly envied the arrogant when he saw the prosperity of the wicked (Ps. 73:2–3)—that is, until he "entered the sanctuary of God; then I understood their final destiny" (v. 17). He realized how silly it was to have jealous thoughts (vv. 19–22).

Here is how you and I can be popular in heaven when it comes to money. First, when we seek God alone. It is choosing His will above all else. Putting Him absolutely first. Keeping our eyes on Jesus. Second, when we are generous in our giving. This begins with the tithe. Those who choose to live on 90 percent of their income are popular in heaven. They also learn that one cannot out-give the Lord (2 Cor. 9:6). Please see my book *Tithing*.[4] Third, when we reject the temptation to be envious at those who have more than we have. This is not easy, especially when it often appears that those people—including Christians—seem to be lukewarm in their love for God but excel in financial blessing. Get over it! It is a test whether we truly value being popular in heaven more than being accepted here on earth.

God is sovereign. He is sovereign in all things. And when it comes to wealth, God decides who will be wealthy. "I will have mercy on whom I will have mercy" (Rom. 9:15) is a verse that applies not only to salvation and inheritance but everything else—who is healed, who is wealthy, who gets married, who gets unusual gifts. Speaking personally, I concluded a long time ago that God does not want me to be wealthy—except to be rich in His grace. God will give me what I *need* in this life. The moment I become discontented with my lack of money, I risk grieving His Spirit. I therefore make a choice! I prefer a greater anointing of the Holy Spirit to greater wealth; I prefer to be popular in heaven than to have a lot of money here below.

My sincere advice: learn to recognize and reject a love for money. Seek after riches and you will be sorry. If you are called to be wealthy, it will come to you with ease. If your anointing—or gifting—is to make a lot of money, it will seem natural and easy. Jackie Pullinger once said to me, "To the spiritual the supernatural seems natural." That would be true with any gift—whether to make money or to heal people.

The great curse on the healing movement became evident when the preachers who prayed for the sick began to emphasize prosperity alongside being healed. This came about partly because fewer and fewer people were being healed, but also because an emphasis on prosperity struck a chord in people's natural greed. It brought in more money to support ministries so many of these preachers gave in to it. Popularity on earth became more satisfying than being popular in heaven. I don't mean to be unfair, but I would not want to be in these preachers' shoes at the judgment seat of Christ for anything in this world. Life is so short, and we will be standing before God before we have time to think about it much. Billy Graham said, "The longer I live the faster time flies."

Being popular in heaven is the better choice than being prosperous on earth. Let God determine your financial situation. He has promised to supply all your need according to His riches in glory (Phil. 4:19). When you stand before God you will be so glad you avoided the love of money.

3. Pride

"Pride goes before destruction, a haughty spirit before a fall" (Prov. 16:18). This is *so* true. Dr. Martyn Lloyd-Jones used to say to me, "The worst thing that can happen to a man is to succeed before he is ready." The reason: pride. If a person rises to an exalted place before he or she is spiritually prepared, the result will almost always be a disaster. King Saul, the prime example of a person who became "yesterday's man," succeeded before he was ready. Success went to his head. He became unteachable and unreachable. He took himself too seriously and refused to play by the rules (1 Sam. 13:9–14).

I remember watching a rising star on a religious TV program a number of years ago. He was an affable young man, but there was something about his spirit that gave me an uneasy feeling. I found out later that things went wrong and he lost the pastorate of his famous church. I never thought I would meet him, but, as it happened, he came to hear me preach at Westminster Chapel. He was clearly keen to get back "on top." I cautioned him not to be in a hurry, quoting the previously mentioned statement by Dr. Martyn Lloyd-Jones. He thanked me and said he agreed. If only. The next thing I knew he was struggling hard to make a name for himself. His second downfall came in a very short period of time. Since then he has tried again to climb back. It is unlikely he will ever reach his former glory.

Immediately after Dr. Lloyd-Jones gave me his caution regarding succeeding before one is ready, I prayed as hard and sincerely as I knew how that God would not let me succeed before I was ready. I have reason to believe that God answered my prayer. Early on in my ministry Dr. Lloyd-Jones also said to me, "You are going to do what I did." I was naturally delighted by that. But the truth is, I never did succeed as he did. And yet I look back on those days with gratitude for the way God led me. For one thing, had I succeeded as Dr. Lloyd-Jones did, I would have never been open to having people such as Arthur Blessitt preach for me. You can always tell a successful man, but you cannot tell him much. Had I succeeded early on as I hoped, I would never have been open to Arthur—not to mention other Spirit-filled men. Having Arthur there was truly the best decision I made in twenty-five years at Westminster Chapel. But there is no doubt in my mind that I would have been too proud to invite him had I seen a Westminster Chapel filled from top to bottom. My disappointment in not seeing a full Westminster Chapel was a puncture to my pride but was one of the best things that ever happened—or didn't happen—to me.

Pride is a feeling of deep pleasure that comes from one's own achievements. It can be a feeling of inward conceit owing to one's good looks, pedigree, intelligence, or connections. I have to tell you, God does not like things like this! "What people value highly is detestable in God's sight" (Luke 16:15). "What is exalted among men is an abomination in the sight of God" (ESV). But pride can be more than that; it is a defense mechanism that keeps us from admitting we are wrong. For example, losing your temper is what gets you into trouble; pride is what keeps you in trouble.

Pride is what makes us protect our reputations—even our future reputations. Presidents want to protect their legacies, to make sure they will be remembered in history in a certain way. That is understandable. But whatever will this mean at the judgment seat of Christ when *the truth* about all people will be revealed? How we will be remembered may seem important now. But what does it matter? All will be revealed when God exposes the secrets of men's hearts at the final judgment (1 Cor. 4:5). Those who most value how they will be remembered are sometimes pitiful failures in this life but still try to salvage their folly. Two men who built monuments to themselves were both utter failures—King Saul (1 Sam. 15:12) and Absalom (2 Sam. 18:18).

Pride is what lies behind the desire to be important and popular.

This is natural and understandable. Of course we care how we are perceived. Why do we comb our hair and dress to look presentable? Of course I care whether I do a good job in writing this very book. But the question we must ask: What is God's opinion in all this?

But you may ask: Is it not pride that wants us to hear Jesus' words, "Well done"? Is it not pride that motivates us to have our names cleared at the judgment seat of Christ? I reply: when it brings glory to God, it is a pride that God Himself honors. That is the essence of being popular in heaven. Should we not take pride in the possibility that we are popular in heaven? Yes. But it is a God-honoring pride and a pursuit in life that gives God pleasure.

I sometimes ask: "What is the greatest feeling in the world? What brings the optimum level of fun and pleasure?" Watching the winners of Wimbledon lie facedown on that green grass when they know they just won the most coveted tennis championship on the planet. Tears fill their eyes—and ours. Or picture this: the person having just won the Gold Medal at the Olympics as he hears his national anthem played. Tears fill his eyes—and ours. But whatever will it be like when we stand before King Jesus and have Him look straight into our eyes and say, "Good. Well done." There cannot possibly be a greater joy, thrill, excitement, or pleasure than this. Knowing you will not only go to heaven but will also enter heaven having been welcomed with a "well done" brings greater joy than can be conceived!

It comes from making the choice to be popular in heaven in our lifetime.

4. Grumbling

If we had any idea how much God hates grumbling, murmuring, griping, whining, carping, and complaining, I feel sure we would stop it. He hates grumbling. It came as a shock to me one day when I saw that God lists grumbling alongside idolatry and sexual promiscuity (1 Cor. 10:7–10). Being unthankful (Rom. 1:21) is part of the list of heinous sins that bring about God's wrath (vv. 28–32). The ancient Gnostics who wanted to destroy the early church were "grumblers" (Jude 16). Paul said that in the last days people would be "ungrateful" (2 Tim. 3:1–2).

Grumbling is angry muttering under our breath about things we don't like. It has been described as complaining in a bad-tempered but muted way. It is to complain sullenly in a low, indistinct sound. Like your stomach growling. It is the sound of bitterness. Bitterness is the chief sin that grieves the Holy Spirit (Eph. 4:30–31). It mirrors an unforgiving and angry heart. And God won't have it!

Grumbling is the opposite of gratitude, thankfulness. God loves gratitude; He hates ingratitude. Grumbling is rooted in unthankfulness and ingratitude. And yet it is the most natural feeling in the world. Like being hurt by someone or lied about, you want vengeance; you want to see that person punished. It does not take a work of the Holy Spirit to pursue vengeance! It is as natural as sexual desire. But as sexual desire must be subordinated to God's commands, so grumbling must be extinguished in us.

> If Jesus Christ be God and died for me, then no sacrifice can be too great for me to make for him.[5]
>
> —C. T. Studd

To be popular in heaven, one must refuse to grumble; remember to be thankful, as we will see further below.

5. Unbelief

When things go wrong, when God suddenly hides His face and does not answer our prayers, and when God allows the most unjust, unfair, and evil thing to happen to us, our immediate reaction is to think that there is no God. Yes, even Christians are faced with this notion. What do you do? You reject it immediately.

Refuse to give it two seconds. This is why the writer of Hebrews states that anyone who comes to God "must believe that he exists" (Heb. 11:6). It may seem strange that the writer of Hebrews would say this to Christians! But he does. And the reason is because it is natural to have this thought. As being betrayed or lied about leaves one with the feeling of wanting vengeance, so when God appears to turn His back on us, we are instantly faced with the thought: "If there were a God, this would not happen." *That is why* the writer says that in coming to God we must believe that He "exists"—or that He "is" (Heb. 11:6, KJV).

The devil is crafty, subtle. He lurks about us day and night—twenty-four hours a day—waiting for an opportunity to bring us down. He exploits every sad moment, every instance when God hides His face, each time something goes wrong—and especially when God does not answer our prayers.

When the temptation comes to think that "there is no God," do not dignify the thought. Don't give in to reason. Let your heart be programmed to reject it entirely. You will be so glad you did this later. In the heat of the battle reject the unbelief that the devil wants you to embrace. Do not give Satan that pleasure.

The title of my book *Totally Forgiving God* has been understandably criticized by some good people. But I make abundantly clear in the book that God is just, pure, and holy, and makes no mistakes; He is not guilty of any wrong! The point is, because God is powerful and *could* stop evil at any moment if He chose to, we must let Him off the hook for His reasons for not doing this.

Without faith it is impossible to please God. But note that the writer has a further word about this—we must never forget it: we must believe that He exists *and* rewards those who "earnestly seek him" (Heb. 11:6). Don't give up. Jesus gave us the parable of the persistent widow to encourage us to pray and never give up or lose heart (Luke 18:1). This is absolutely and totally and faithfully true. Those who seek Him—and break the betrayal barrier—prove to be sovereign vessels. He will not desert *anybody* who earnestly seeks Him. Don't give up. "Never, never, never...never give in"—as Winston Churchill said in the heat of World War II.[6]

Do you want to be popular in heaven? Reject any hint of unbelief. Nip it in the bud when the temptation to not believe comes. This honors God and pays incalculable dividends down the road.

Chapter 5

THE HONOR AND PRAISE OF GOD

How can you believe, who receive honor from one another, and do not seek the honor that comes from the only God?

—John 5:44, NKJV

For more than sixty years John 5:44 has been my life verse. By that I mean I have *sought* to be governed by this principle: seeking God's honor rather than man's. I do not say I have always succeeded in doing this. Too often I have been influenced by the approval of people and the fear of man. The fear of man will always prove to be a "snare"—so true; but whoever trusts in the Lord will be kept safe (Prov. 29:25). Or as the *New Living Translation* puts it, "Fearing people is a dangerous trap, but trusting the Lord means safety." Fearing people is the devil's trap to keep you and me from receiving the blessing from God that would come to us by choosing the people's approval.

Pursuing the principle of John 5:44 is the best antidote to keep us from being governed by the fear of people and lead us to being popular in heaven.

Why the Jews Missed Their Messiah

John 5:44 is directed to the Jews generally and, almost certainly, the Pharisees particularly. The Pharisees were a prominent sect in ancient Judaism. They considered themselves not only to be experts in the Mosaic Law but fancied themselves to be a cut above all other Jews—whether these Jews be Sadducees, scribes, or zealots. The Sadducees were made up mostly of priestly families. They were more prestigious but fewer in number than the Pharisees. A real rivalry existed between the Sadducees and Pharisees (see Matthew 22:34, for example). That said, verses that precede John 5:44 (verses 5:1, 10, 15–16, and 18) merely refer to "Jews," but these would probably refer to Pharisees if not also the other groups. (See John 1:24; 3:1; 4:1, which show Pharisees being mentioned in the fourth Gospel prior to John 5.)

My point is this. John 5:44 contains a question—a question that cannot really be answered. How do you answer a question like that? Likewise Jesus asks a question implicitly to all Jews that is almost impossible to answer: "How *can* you believe that I am the promised Messiah?" Jesus knew they did not believe that He was the promised Messiah. So when Jesus asks the question, the answer assumes an implicit conclusion: *You cannot believe. You are not able to believe.* It is as though Jesus implicitly answers the question by the way He framed the question: "Surprise, surprise, you are *unable* to believe!"

The reason therefore they were unable to believe is because they *made no attempt* to obtain the honor that comes from the only God. It was not on their radar screen to seek the honor and approval and opinion of God. It should have been. Had the Jews in Jesus' day been in a good place spiritually, they would have *wanted* the honor of God. Had the honor and praise of God been of paramount importance to them, they would not have missed what God was doing in their day. Jonathan Edwards (1703–1758) taught us that the task of every generation is to discover in which direction the Sovereign Redeemer is moving, then move in that direction. The clear direction of the Sovereign Redeemer two thousand years ago was sending His Son to His own people, the Jews. Jesus came to His own people, but His own did not receive Him (John 1:11). Sadly they only wanted approval from one another; that was all that mattered to them. For this reason, the Jews shut off, closed down, any conduit or channel by which they would be able to discern what God was doing before their eyes. God's sense of approval of them was consequently forfeited. They therefore lost the opportunity to believe in their promised Messiah.

Had they been devoted to God's honor, then, they would not have missed recognizing Jesus as God's promised Messiah. But they did miss Him, they missed Him entirely, and forfeited the praise and approval that would have come from the only true God.

In other words, the Jews in Jesus' day made a choice to be popular with people. All they did was done for people to see (Matt. 23:5). If they gave to the poor or fasted and prayed, they did it in order to be admired by people (Matt. 6:1–18). It did not cross their minds to do these things only to honor God.

Therefore when you and I make choices like they made, we forfeit being popular in heaven. Also like them, it means we might miss out entirely on seeing God work. But we do not need to repeat their folly.

Why John 5:44 Is So Important

You've probably begun to see why John 5:44 is so important. For the rest of this chapter I'm going to dive into the five key reasons why this verse makes all the difference.

1. It shows the reason that the people of God, the Jews, missed their Messiah.

I have people ask me from time to time: How could the Jews have missed their Messiah? Some readers will know I have written a book with Rabbi Sir David Rosen called *The Christian and the Pharisee* (his choice for a title).[1] Some readers were amazed that David, a lovely man and good friend, could not see what I was stating. But the conclusion was, he turned out to be very like the original Pharisees in Jesus' day! He nullifies the Word of God by his tradition (Mark 7:13). When Christians read Old Testament passages, such as Isaiah 53, it is so obvious that these verses referred to Jesus. It seems extraordinary, then, that the Jews would not see this! For example:

> He had no beauty or majesty to attract us to him,
> nothing in his appearance that we should desire him.
> He was despised and rejected by mankind,
> a man of suffering, and familiar with pain.
> Like one from whom people hide their faces
> he was despised, and we held him in low esteem...
> Yet we considered him punished by God,
> stricken by him, and afflicted.
> But he was pierced for our transgressions,
> he was crushed for our iniquities...
> and the Lord has laid on him
> the iniquity of us all.
> He was oppressed and afflicted,
> yet he did not open his mouth;
> he was led like a lamb to the slaughter,
> and as a sheep before its shearers is silent,
> so he did not open his mouth.
>
> —Isaiah 53:2–7

If you were to insert *Jesus* each time Isaiah refers to "he" or "him," right through the end of Isaiah 53, you would see how this makes perfect sense. You could also insert "the Jews" when you read the word "we" or "us" in these verses. Please also see my book *Why Jesus Died* (my treatment of Isaiah 53).[2] It is *so* obvious the prophet Isaiah is talking about Jesus.

But they were blind. They could not see what God was doing. They were stone-deaf. They could not hear God speak. All because the honor of God was not in their hearts. Had the honor of God been their priority they would have recognized who Jesus was.

There was not a Pharisee or Sadducee who thought that the Messiah could come along and they miss Him! How often had rabbis quoted Isaiah 64:1 in synagogues all over Galilee and Judea: "Oh that you would rend the heavens and come down." They confidentially assumed, "We will be the first to recognize the Messiah. There is no way Messiah could come and we not see Him." But when He came down, they did not recognize Him.

2. It demonstrates how the people of God today—professing Christians—still miss the current move of the Holy Spirit.

When we did some controversial things at Westminster Chapel—like having Arthur Blessitt (the man who has carried the cross all over the globe) preach for us—a fellow minister in London wrote me a letter. Slapping me on the wrist, he said, "When revival comes to London, I'll know it." He himself had written and preached a lot on the subject of revival and assumed he was a bit of an expert on this subject, not unlike the Pharisees and Sadducees who assumed they would recognize God's Messiah.

I often think of the British missionaries in India who heard that revival had broken out in Wales in 1904. They got on a ship heading for England. After landing in Southampton and coming up to London they ran into some old friends.

Their friends said to them, "What are you doing here? We thought you were in India."

They replied, "We are going to Wales. We want to see the revival that has broken out there."

Their friends then said to them, "Don't bother. It is Welsh emotionalism."

"Oh, thanks for telling us," was the response. The couple took the next ship to India and missed one of the great moves of the Holy Spirit in church history—the Welsh Revival! All because they did not want to offend their friends!

Every true revival carries a stigma with it. The stigma—the offense that comes down to the word *embarrassment*—is what brings the "antis" together. Once this bond is made, people don't want to break ranks and offend anyone. Just like the Jews who missed Jesus.

When I invited Arthur Blessitt to preach for us for six weeks in the spring of 1982, one deacon was offended. It was an amazing six weeks. Arthur got us doing things unprecedented at Westminster Chapel—singing choruses (not only traditional hymns), inviting people publicly to receive Christ (but never using pressure), and witnessing on the streets, which gave birth to our Pilot Light ministry. Having had thirty-five years to think about it, more than ever I regard having him as the best decision I made in our twenty-five years there. That is, apart from my learning total forgiveness.

But the offended deacon found a fellow deacon and convinced him that I was leading the Chapel in the wrong direction. Within a year there were three deacons against us. By the autumn of 1984 there were four deacons (out of twelve) against my ministry. By Christmas there were six! On the Sunday before Christmas 1984 these six deacons composed a letter that was sent to the entire membership—accusing me of false doctrine. What they accused me of was exactly what I preached for four years—from my first day there—when no one said a word against my preaching. Indeed, these same men loved me in those days. We had tremendous unity from my arrival in 1977 to May 1982. But when the offense of the altar call, witnessing in Buckingham Gate, and singing contemporary songs set in, they turned their opposition into a theological issue. That is the first time I heard the expression "antis." In those hard days—the worst experience of my life—people were either for my ministry or "anti." In any case, at a historic church meeting—January 16, 1985—the church overwhelmingly dismissed these six deacons.

I am not saying that true revival came to Westminster Chapel during my time there. But I will say that a touch of the Holy Spirit was present during the ministry of Arthur Blessitt and our remaining years there—including our being exposed to prophetic ministry and the Toronto Blessing. Most of all, we were totally committed to evangelism. It was all about seeing the lost come to Jesus Christ.

Do I believe that we were popular in heaven in those days? Yes. That alone was what kept us going.

3. John 5:44 shows the reason we forfeit hearing from God, and likewise forfeit receiving the knowledge of His will.

Behind this verse is the implicit Old Testament teaching of the jealousy of God. God does not like it one bit when we seek approval of one another over seeking His approval.

John 5:44 is a formula for intimacy with God. If we are addicted to man's approval, we unwittingly shut off intimacy with the Holy Spirit. Never forget that *the Holy Spirit is God* and is a jealous God (Exod. 34:14). When we are in bondage to the need to be popular with people, we close down the channel by which we hear from God.

I sincerely hope you want to hear from God—to know His will. If so, be very aware that you cannot have it both ways. You make a choice to be popular with people to avoid a stigma, or to be popular in heaven, which means bearing a stigma on earth.

This is why we have the admonition, "If you hear his voice"

(Heb. 3:7, quoting Ps. 95:7). The ancient Hebrews did not hear God's voice because they had ceased to desire the honor and glory of God. The Hebrew Christians, to whom the Epistle to the Hebrews was written, were in grave danger of repeating the folly of what their forefathers had done. These Jewish believers had already become "dull of hearing" (Heb. 5:11, ESV). The worst scenario would be to become stone-deaf to hearing God—when you can hear nothing at all from Him. Those who degenerated into stone-deafness, though they had previously experienced God in an amazing manner, were not able to be renewed again (Greek *palin*) to repentance (Heb. 6:4–6). (See my book *Are You Stone Deaf to the Spirit or Rediscovering God?*[3])

4. It shows the basis on which we receive a reward at the judgment seat of Christ.

> For we must all appear before the judgment seat of Christ, so that each of us may receive what is due us for the things done while in the body, whether good or bad.
>
> —2 Corinthians 5:10

All Christians—as well as non-Christians—will stand before God on the day of judgment. "People are destined to die once, and after that to face judgment" (Heb. 9:27). The unsaved will be shown how true justice will lead to their eternal condemnation. They will go to "eternal punishment, the righteous to eternal life" (Matt. 25:46). All Christians too will stand before God. Some will receive a reward at the judgment seat of Christ, some won't. Those who don't receive a reward *will be saved*—but by fire (1 Cor. 3:15). All Christians are called to enter into their inheritance. Some do, some don't. Those who were faithfully pursuing their inheritance—which makes them popular in heaven—will receive a reward. There are at least four words that may be used interchangeably: *inheritance* (Col. 3:24), *reward* (1 Cor. 3:14), *prize* (1 Cor. 9:24; Phil. 3:14), and *crown* (1 Cor. 9:25; 2 Tim. 4:8).

This crown, reward, inheritance, or prize was very important to Paul. He had this in mind when he said: "I strike a blow to my body and make it my slave so that after I have preached to others, I myself will not be disqualified for the prize" (1 Cor. 9:27). Paul was not speaking about whether he will make it to heaven. Heaven is a given once we have come to Christ in faith. He was therefore never worried about whether he would go to heaven. But he was concerned at that time whether he himself would receive the prize or crown. First Corinthians was written probably around AD 55. He was still pressing for the prize when he wrote Philippians 3:14: "I press on toward the goal to win the prize." That was likely in AD 62. But by the time he wrote his final letter to Timothy, probably in AD 65, he no longer worried whether he would get the prize. He was waiting for his execution any day:

> I have fought the good fight, I have finished the race, I have kept the faith. Now there is in store for me the crown of righteousness, which the Lord, the righteous Judge, will award to me on that day—and not only to me, but also to all who have longed for his appearing.
>
> —2 Timothy 4:7–8

If you ask, "What exactly is the prize?" I answer: I don't know. But if it is receiving the Lord's "well done," that is good enough for me.

One might have thought that, surely, Paul was assured of this prize in AD 55 when he wrote his first letter to the Corinthians. But no. He had years left. He was presuming nothing! He waited until just before he would be taken to heaven to claim the prize. Temptation, as we saw earlier, includes sex, money, pride, complaining, and unbelief. The truth is, we will fight temptation at all levels throughout our lives.

In other words, the "prize" at the judgment seat of Christ would be receiving this same aforementioned praise or honor from the only God. That is the highest honor ever conceived. It is worth seeking after in this life and certainly worth waiting for.

Perhaps one of the most amazing examples of someone who spent his lifetime seeking only to "press toward the goal to win the prize" of God's praise and honor in heaven was a humble Christian man from Sydney, Australia, named Mr. Jenner (commonly spelled Genor). As a young man, he served as a seaman on an Australian warship. In his own words he says: "I lived a reprobate life." But when a devastating crisis happened to him, he hit a wall. In desperation he sought help from a fellow seaman, who happened to be a Christian. Although he says he "gave literal hell" to his helper, the seaman led him to Jesus. The change in Mr. Jenner's life in just a twenty-four-hour period was truly amazing.[4]

That very day he made a promise to God that he would share Jesus in a simple witness with at least ten people every day. He tells of his efforts, "Sometimes I was ill, I couldn't do it, but I made up for it other times. I wasn't paranoid about it. But I have done this for over forty years, and in my retirement years the best place was on George Street. There were hundreds of people. I got lots of rejections, but a lot of people courteously took the tracts." Mr. Jenner found no reward for his efforts on earth. In his forty years of faithful witnessing on George Street, he never heard of one single person coming to Jesus.[5]

But fortunately his story didn't end there. In the span of three short years, one Baptist pastor in southern London became overwhelmed as he heard over and over of Mr. Jenner's efforts. He relates the stories of these evidences of Mr. Jenner's faithfulness with this first example: At the close of a Sunday morning service in his church, a stranger asked to share a testimony. The pastor said, "You've got three minutes."

The stranger continued: "I just moved into this area. I used to live in another part of London. I came from Sydney, Australia. Just a few months back I was visiting some relatives, and I was walking down George Street….A strange little white-haired man stepped out of a shop doorway, put a pamphlet in my hand and said, 'Excuse me, are you saved? If you died tonight, are you going to heaven?' I was astounded by those words. Nobody had ever told me that. I thanked him courteously, and all the way on British Airlines back to Heathrow this puzzled me. I called a friend who lived in this new area where I am living now. And thank God, he was a Christian, he led me to Christ. I am a Christian, and I want to fellowship here."[6]

During the next three years, the Baptist pastor heard over and over again about the little white-haired man on George Street who handed out tracts and asked, "Are you saved? If you died tonight, are you going to heaven?"

- When the pastor was ministering in Adelaide, Australia, a woman came to him for counseling. She told him that on a trip to Sydney, Mr. Jenner had witnessed to her with his questions. She returned home, sought out a pastor, and was led to Christ as a result.

- While the pastor was ministering in Perth, a senior elder took him out for a meal. The pastor asked him how he got saved. The elder told him that although he attended church faithfully, he had never made a commitment to Jesus. One night on a business trip to Sydney years earlier, he met Mr. Jenner on George Street. He tried to explain to Mr. Jenner that he was a Baptist elder after all, but Mr. Jenner still pressed him with the questions. Upset by the experience, when he got back home the elder told his pastor that he knew he didn't have a relationship with Jesus, and the pastor led him to Jesus that day.

- At another speaking engagement, four elderly pastors told the London pastor they had all been impacted by Mr. Jenner's witness more than twenty-five and thirty-five years earlier, and each was saved as a result.

- Many years prior, three missionaries from the Caribbean attended a conference in Sydney, Australia, and each had become a Christian after meeting Mr. Jenner. They went on to become missionaries in the Caribbean.

- During a Naval Chaplain Soul Winning Convention in Atlanta, Georgia, the chaplain general shared his own story. As a young sailor, he lived a wild, sinful life. When his ship docked in Sydney, Australia, one night he took the wrong bus while blind drunk and landed on George Street. When Mr. Jenner jumped in front of him, pushed a tract in his hand, and asked, "Sailor, are you saved? If you died tonight would you go to heaven?" he said the fear of God hit him, and he was shocked sober. That night the ship's chaplain led him to the Lord, and he immediately began to prepare for the ministry and was now in charge of more than a thousand naval chaplains who were all bent on soul winning.

- During a convention for five thousand Indian missionaries in a remote corner of northeastern India,

> the humble little Indian missionary in charge told the pastor his story. As a younger man he was in a privileged position with the Indian Diplomatic Mission. He traveled the world, living a very sinful life. One night while shopping on George Street in Sydney, Australia, Mr. Jenner stopped him and asked him the life-changing questions. As a Hindu, the man was confused by the questions, and when he got home, he sought advice from the Hindu priest. The priest suggested that just to satisfy his curiosity, he talk with the Christian missionary who lived at the end of the street. He did and the missionary led him to Christ. He quit Hinduism, left the diplomatic service, became a missionary, and was now in charge of the five thousand missionaries at this convention, who together were leading hundreds of thousands of Indians to Christ.

At the end of this three-year span, the London pastor was ministering in Sydney. A Baptist minister there knew of the work of Mr. Jenner and was able to take the pastor to see him in his little Sydney apartment. After forty long years of faithful witnessing on George Street, Mr. Jenner was finally able to hear that his ministry had indeed been fruitful. Tears flowed down his face as the pastor told the stories of those who had spoken to him of the meetings on George Street.

Through those stories alone, the London pastor was able to determine that the faithful, simple little Christian man had influenced at least 146,100 people for Jesus. And he believed that was just the tip of the iceberg of influence. Only God knew how many more individuals had been arrested for Christ and were doing huge jobs out in the mission field.

The narrating pastor explained: "Mr. Jenner died two weeks

later. Can you imagine the reward he went home to in heaven? I doubt that his face ever appeared on *Charisma* magazine. I doubt if there had ever been a write-up with a photograph in Billy Graham's *Decision Magazine*, as beautiful as those magazines are. Nobody except a little group of Baptists in southern Sydney knew about that Mr. Jenner. But I tell you this; his name was famous in heaven. Heaven knew Mr. Jenner. And you can imagine the welcome and the red carpet and the fanfare he received when he arrived in glory."[7]

5. John 5:44 allows for a subtle distinction between seeking God's praise and consciously achieving it.

Jesus does not tell us whether God's praise is to be received only at the judgment seat of Christ or if one might consciously obtain it here below. At least in measure. What we know for sure is this. The Pharisees "made no attempt" to seek after the praise of God. This would have made them unpopular among the Jews. To be popular in heaven would come to those who make every effort to obtain His praise by eschewing the praise of people here below.

The question is, Can one consciously receive the praise of God while we are still on our earthly journey? That would mean knowing now that we are popular in heaven. So can we know we are popular in heaven? Yes.

God may give us increments of His praise below. It comes by passing tests as we go along. That we pass a test along the way does not guarantee we will keep pursuing His glory. But it is a good sign. At any rate, one must keep on keeping on!

I was given a test during the days I was selling vacuum cleaners. Those were hard days. I sold vacuum cleaners door-to-door for a total of six years. There were times when I wondered if I would ever be in full-time ministry again. This was because I was *so* deep in debt in those days. I wondered now and then if I had missed it along the way. One of my customers was Nathan Darsky, a Russian Jew who came to America at an early age. He was a founder of Pepsi Cola Co., and God gave me favor with him. So much so that he invited me to offer a prayer of invocation at the beginning of a huge banquet. It was to be held in the prestigious Fontainebleau hotel in Miami Beach. The movie star Joan Crawford, the chairman of the board of Pepsi Cola, was to be there. Mr. Darsky would be honored. My wife, Louise, and I were to be seated at the head table with Mr. Darsky and Joan Crawford. It was an exciting honor for someone like me—unknown and without a future except for promises of God. But a week before the banquet Mr. Darsky phoned and asked me, "What are you going to say in your prayer?" The truth is, I had given it no thought. But he asked me to give him some of the prayer. I repeated certain lines that seemed appropriate: "Heavenly Father, thank You for this occasion. Thank You for blessing Pepsi Cola. Thank You for Mr. Nathan Darsky," and things like that. He echoed approval with each of those lines. That is, until I came to the end of the prayer, and I said: "In Jesus' name. Amen."

He quickly asked, "Must you bring in that last part?"

"Yes, of course," I replied.

"There will be a lot of Jewish people there. They may not like that part of your prayer," he added.

"But Mr. Darsky," I reminded him, "I always pray in Jesus' name when I pray with you. You must have heard that several times."

"I know, I know, but some of my family may not be happy with that."

He promised to come back to me soon. He did. He seemed to be very sad to say, "I am sorry, but I have been overruled. Will you please leave out praying in 'Jesus' name'?"

"No, I'm also sorry, Mr. Darsky, but I must always pray in Jesus' name," I replied.

And yet I look back on that occasion and regard it as a test from heaven. Would I be popular with Mr. Darsky's friends and relatives and meet famous people? Or be popular in heaven? After all, who on earth would ever find out if I simply closed the prayer "In Your name. Amen" or "In God's name. Amen" or simply, "Amen"?

But all heaven would know.

To be totally honest, it wasn't really all that hard to say no to Mr. Darsky. I would not have left out Jesus' name in that prayer for a million dollars. And yet I still think it was a test from God—if only to let me see for myself where I stood on an issue like this.

I see this incident as an illustration of how one can sense he or she is popular in heaven.

Chapter 6

WHAT IS UNPOPULAR IN HEAVEN?

You are the ones who justify yourselves in the eyes of others, but God knows your hearts. What people value highly is detestable in God's sight.

—Luke 16:15

Probably the most neglected teaching of Jesus is what He has to say about hell and eternal punishment. But the most underestimated *feeling* of Jesus is His attitude toward sin today. Equally overlooked is His present opinion of what is going on in His church.

In this generation of "What's in it for me?" we tend to see Jesus as what we want Him to be—kind, loving, gentle, humble, meek, fully human, and lowly—mirroring the Father's tenderness. Yes, you can be sure He is all these things. But He is equally impartial, fearless, fully aware, observant, changeless, fully God, and mirrors the Father's wrath.

This surprises some people. It shouldn't. The same Jesus who chased the money changers out of the temple with a whip—showing His anger toward abuse of worship (John 2:13–16;

Mark 11:15–17)—is the One John saw on the Isle of Patmos who had eyes like "blazing fire" and feet like "bronze glowing in a furnace" (Rev. 1:14–15). Jesus Christ is the same "yesterday and today and forever" (Heb. 13:8). Also often forgotten are the words of this same Jesus from the right hand of God to the seven churches in Asia.

> If you do not repent, I will come to you and remove your lampstand from its place.
>
> —Revelation 2:5

> Repent therefore! Otherwise, I will soon come to you and will fight against them with the sword of my mouth.
>
> —Revelation 2:16

> I will cast her on a bed of suffering, and I will make those who commit adultery with her suffer intensely, unless they repent of her ways.
>
> —Revelation 2:22

> I know your deeds; you have a reputation of being alive, but you are dead. Wake up! Strengthen what remains and is about to die, for I have found your deeds unfinished in the sight of my God. Remember, therefore, what you have received and heard; hold it fast, and repent. But if you do not wake up, I will come like a thief, and you will not know at what time I will come to you.
>
> —Revelation 3:1–3

> Because you are lukewarm—neither hot nor cold—I am about to spit you out of my mouth.
>
> —Revelation 3:16

These observations of Jesus show us how aware He is of what is going on in His church on the earth. He knows everything. The

Book of Revelation among other things unveils how Jesus *feels* about what is going on in His church.

With these words above quoted, do not forget also the way in which our Lord Jesus Christ revealed His total awareness, sympathy, and approval of what was going on in parts of His church. These words also show not only that Jesus knows everything, but also that He is aware of our faithfulness.

> I know your deeds, your hard work and perseverance. I know that you cannot tolerate wicked people, that you have tested those who claim to be apostles but are not, and have found them false. You have persevered and have endured hardships for my name, and have not grown weary.
>
> —REVELATION 2:2–3

> I know your afflictions and your poverty—yet you are rich! I know the slander of those who say they are Jews and are not, but are a synagogue of Satan. Do not be afraid of what you are about to suffer.... Be faithful, even to the point of death, and I will give you life as your victor's crown.
>
> —REVELATION 2:9–10

> I know where you live—where Satan has his throne. Yet you remain true to my name. You did not renounce your faith in me, even in the days of Antipas, my faithful witness, who was put to death in your city—where Satan lives.
>
> —REVELATION 2:13

> I know your deeds, your love and faith, your service and perseverance, and that you are now doing more than you did at first.
>
> —REVELATION 2:19

> You have a few people in Sardis who have not soiled their clothes. They will walk with me, dressed in white, for they are worthy.
>
> —Revelation 3:4

> I have placed before you an open door that no one can shut. I know that you have little strength, yet you have kept my word and have not denied my name. I will make those who are of the synagogue of Satan, who claim to be Jews though they are not, but are liars—I will make them come and fall down at your feet and acknowledge that I have loved you. Since you have kept my command to endure patiently, I will also keep you from the hour of trial that is going to come on the whole world to test the inhabitants of the earth. I am coming soon. Hold on to what you have, so that no one will take your crown.
>
> —Revelation 3:8–11

> Those whom I love I rebuke and discipline.
>
> —Revelation 3:19

For approximately six months in 1956 I had a series of visions. I don't have them today, and in some ways I'm glad I don't. But for a while I was given visions—some fulfilled, some unfulfilled, and some still a mystery. A few of them enabled me to see what I would call God's opinion of certain people and situations.

Some readers will have read of my experience with the Holy Spirit on October 31, 1955. I will not repeat it here (you can read about this in my book *Holy Fire*[1]), only to say that it was my baptism with the Holy Spirit. The person of Jesus was real to me—*more* real, if this is possible, than anything I now see outside my hotel window as I write these lines. I saw His face on that October day looking at me with tender, languid eyes. This lasted for less than a minute, perhaps for thirty seconds. However, there were a few times—not many but a few—when I would see His face again. It would not come at will but only when He unexpectedly revealed His face. On one occasion I was given to see the Lord's happy approval of a particular person, on two occasions I was shown His disapproval.

I now share two stories that I have never written of before and shared with only one or two people in the past sixty-two years. It happened when I was pastor of my first church—in Palmer, Tennessee, when I was twenty years old. I was simultaneously a student at Trevecca Nazarene College (now a university). My revered district superintendent came to my church unexpectedly one Sunday morning. I was thrilled to see him and delighted that he offered to preach the sermon. He was a man I admired like I have looked up to very few people. He was "next to God" in my eyes. He was highly respected by *all* I knew. All my church members in Palmer stood in awe of him. Years before I had my picture taken with him when he was the preacher at our summer camp meeting in Kentucky. I had the photo enlarged and put on my wall in my room in Ashland, Kentucky. It is impossible to exaggerate how highly I esteemed this man. He and his wife, whom I also knew, died over forty years ago.

As this man was speaking in my church in Palmer that morning, there appeared before my eyes the same face of Jesus. It was an open vision. It was not a dream. I was wide awake; I saw everybody around me as well as the face of Jesus at the same time. This time, however, He was not looking at me but right at the district superintendent as he was speaking—but with a look of intense disapproval. A frown. In anger. In fact I cannot adequately describe the appearance of disapproval; it was a look of disgust.

I was stunned. Sobered. Perplexed. How could this be? Was I being deceived? I kept this to myself for many years, never telling a single soul.

It was revealed some ten years later that my district superintendent was caught having an affair with a woman not far from

Palmer. It would seem that this affair was but one of several. Such were almost certainly going on during the time he came to my church. He was later forced to leave the ministry and died a few years later in disgrace.

Why I was given this vision is still a mystery to me. I can only speculate as to the reason. As best as I can figure out, it was an indication of how a person could be very popular here below—and deceive people generally—but be unpopular in heaven. Like some in the church of Sardis, this preacher had a reputation of "being alive" but was dead (Rev. 3:1). I would have to say that this man was certainly unpopular in heaven by the look I saw on Jesus' face. That look has also made me think of John's vision of Jesus with eyes like fire (Rev. 1:14). John's revelation shows Jesus' anger with sin.

The other occasion of a similar open vision was during a class at Trevecca. A lady professor there taught French and other languages. She was a well-known linguist who could read over twenty languages, including ancient Egyptian hieroglyphics. She was also esteemed as a very godly woman. I admired her greatly. But one day during a class I had virtually the same vision as the one of my district superintendent. There was Jesus looking at her with intense disapproval. I could not understand it. I tried hard to dismiss it and managed to put it behind me. She too died many years ago. But only two years ago—this would mean some sixty years later—a former official of Trevecca revealed to me that this woman had been involved in a lesbian affair while at Trevecca. I wondered why I had that vision that many years ago and still do.

My only conclusion is that these two visions indicate how people can be highly esteemed here on this earth but not in heaven. I would have to say that these two visions show that there are people who must be very *unpopular in heaven.* These visions suggest that there must be countless situations on earth in which a person may be very popular on earth—in a church, a family, a school, in government, or in politics—and be very unpopular in heaven.

God's Opinion

I wonder how many times I have seen people whom I admired but never connected with a vision of Jesus in order to know God's opinion of them. Countless people, of course, thousands, tens of thousands, maybe even millions. If God were pleased to do so, He could let me discern His opinion of every single person I run into! I suppose some prophetic people have this gift. God has mercifully chosen not to let me have visions like this in over sixty years.

But the truth is, He has an *opinion* of every single person I meet. Every person I see at a distance, shake hands with, or get close to. Yes, God has an opinion of every one of them. It is possible I have had many friends that Jesus' face would reveal disapproval of. It is also possible I have enemies that would have His approval! It is surely good that He has not let me see His opinion. It would give me information I could probably not cope with. But the fact remains, God does have an opinion of every person. What is more, what matters is not how they are regarded by us on earth but how they are regarded by God in heaven.

Here is the most disquieting news of all. One day God will reveal His opinion of every single one of us: "He will bring to light what is hidden in darkness and will expose the motives of the heart" (1 Cor. 4:5).

The word *praise* or *honor* in John 5:44 comes from the Greek word *doxa*—from which we get the doxology: "Praise God from whom all blessings flow." The root word of *doxa* means opinion. That gets to the heart of the meaning: *God's glory is His opinion.* If we want the honor of God we must esteem His opinion more than the praise of people.

God has an opinion on everything. Everything! Had you

thought of that? The question is, "Do we *want* His opinion?" The problem is we are afraid of what His opinion might be! It could go against ours—our plans for the future, a vacation, a job, an ambition, who to vote for in an election, who to spend time with, whether to accept an invitation, or what to do next. God has a point of view on every single thing on earth.

The Pharisees were esteemed on earth, but they were unpopular in heaven. Two thousand years ago ordinary people were in awe of the prestigious Sadducees. But they were not highly esteemed in heaven.

These words of Jesus to the Pharisees in Luke 16:15 are among the most disturbing comments in Holy Scripture. They trouble me!

> He said to them, "You are the ones who justify yourselves in the eyes of others, but God knows your hearts. What people value highly is detestable in God's sight."

Think about this: what is highly esteemed here on earth is detestable in God's sight. This cannot mean literally everything that people on earth esteem. People esteem the beauty of nature—a glorious sunset, the Grand Canyon, the Swiss Alps, the Rocky Mountains, the Smoky Mountains, a babbling brook, the four seasons, a gentle breeze, the rolling tides of the ocean. God esteems His creation too. But Luke 16:15—which corresponds to John 5:44—refers to what people esteem that is *worldly*. We saw what worldliness is in chapter 3.

But Jesus said these threatening words to the Pharisees who, according to Luke, "loved money" and were "sneering at Jesus" (Luke 16:14). Jesus had just said, "No one can serve two masters. Either you will hate the one and love the other, or you will be devoted to the one and despise the other. You cannot serve both God and money" (v. 13). From this we can deduce that what is an abomination in God's sight is in some way connected to:

1. People's love of money
2. A person's self-righteousness
3. People living for one another's approval

This to me suggests that the awe people have for wealthy people, famous people, and well-connected people is unpopular in heaven. Wealthy people often like to shove their weight around. Famous people enjoy ordinary people looking up to them. Well-connected people love it when people bow and scrape to them.

But God hates it. This should have an effect on us lest we be awed by the millionaires of this world, the movie stars, the pop singers, the sports heroes, the politicians. This does not mean that people like this cannot be genuine Christians. But God is displeased when we get silly over the possibility of meeting them or seeing them—knowing how frail, superficial, blind, and unworthy they are! And yet I must come clean here. I was in awe when I met Joe DiMaggio. But the saying is so true: "The best of men are men at best."

Social Sins

My ministry over the years has not largely focused on what are called "social sins." These are sins that are rampant in society. That has not been my calling. So far my emphasis has mainly centered on preaching and teaching—the doctrine of salvation, evangelism, and one's personal Christian life. I have close friends—such as Lyndon Bowring, Clive Calver, Rob Parsons, James Dobson, and others—who have been called to focus on these. But I do feel compelled to deal with some of these issues now in this book.

All social sins are unpopular in heaven, of course, but I will give only a few examples of those that are most prominent at the present time. Keep in mind that Jesus' eyes, like a flame of fire, gaze on these sins with deep vengeance.

Abortions and the lackadaisical attitude some Christians have toward them.

I have been in the office of James Dobson and watched him weep like a child over the incalculable number of abortions in America. He sees his own ministry as saving lives of the unborn.

There have been a staggering 58.5 million babies aborted in the womb in America since January 22, 1973—the date the Supreme Court verdict known as *Roe v. Wade* was handed down. And the number continues to grow. This means 58.5 million murders for which no one will be judged. So far. Abortions worldwide have taken more lives than all the wars, terrorism, and murders carried out by the hands of humanity over the last fifty years. There are approximately 125,000 abortions per day in the United States.[2] Every day in England and Wales more than 500 abortions take place.[3] But mark it down: what is unpopular in heaven will one day be revealed openly. It is when "God judges people's secrets through Jesus Christ" (Rom. 2:16).

The proof that the fetus is a human being is made clear when the baby leaped in Elizabeth's womb when she met the Virgin Mary a day or two after Mary conceived (Luke 1:34–45). Mary paid her visit to Elizabeth immediately—like in a couple days. This shows not only that the baby who became John the Baptist was a human being, but also that the baby who became Jesus was a human being after two days in the womb! A thousand years prior to these holy events David said:

> I praise you because I am fearfully and wonderfully made; your works are wonderful, I know that full well. My frame was not hidden from you when I was made in the secret place, when I was woven together in the depths of the earth. Your eyes saw my unformed body.
>
> —Psalm 139:14–16

Pornography

Possibly the largest-growing addiction in Britain and America, pornography hurts adults, children, couples, families, and societies. Among adolescents it hinders the development of a healthy sexuality, and among adults it distorts sexual attitudes and social realities. Forty million Americans regularly visit porn sites.[4] Twenty-five percent of all search engine queries are related to pornography.[5] One-third of porn viewers are women.[6] Pornography use increases the infidelity rate by 300 percent.[7] In the United Kingdom 75 percent of Christian men view pornography at least once a month.[8] Forty-two percent of UK Christian men admit to being addicted to pornography.[9] Thirty percent of church leaders view porn regularly.[10] The statistics are even more staggering in the United States. According to a recent Barna Group study, 64 percent of Christian men and 15 percent of Christian women admitted to viewing pornography at least once a month.[11]

Sometimes called "the preachers' sin," pornography is an epidemic that has caused marriages to disintegrate and often leaves the participant without a sense of worth. Watching pornography is committing adultery in one's heart—lusting after a woman (Matt. 5:28).

One reason that pornography destroys marriages is that one's wife often becomes less exciting. The person grows to prefer pornography to actual sex with his own wife. It also intensifies the attraction of another woman and often leads to physical adultery.

Those who indulge in pornography are unpopular in heaven. They may feel it is harmless—that "no one knows"—but God knows.

Racism

Racism is hatred or intolerance toward another race or races. Racial prejudice is one of the most inexcusable but common sins in the world today. I call it inexcusable because no one has a choice whether he or she will be born red, yellow, black, or white. We cannot help it that we were born when or where we were—or born with our color. Common sense should stop a person from being biased toward another person owing to their skin color. But we live in a wicked world where common sense does not prevail. To hate some people or someone—or show any measure of disdain toward another human being owing to the color of his or her skin—is so wrong. God hates it. And yet racism pervades in the church—even among many Evangelicals. It is unthinkable, but yet is so common.

What is also so common is the way some white Christians have felt toward black leaders who have tried to lead their people to a level of dignity and honor. I am thinking of the Martin Luther Kings and the Nelson Mandelas of this world who were hated by countless American and South African Christians. Such leaders may not have been perfect in every way, but what they did took great courage and grace. These things said, we need leaders today more than ever—in the church as well as in political leadership—who will take the lead in combatting racism. There will be no racism in heaven. Why must we have it now—especially in the church?

The way I see it, the practice of total forgiveness is the only way forward. But no one, it seems, wants to take the lead. But if our Christian faith would go deep enough in all of us, racial hatred could come to an end. My best-known sermon—and book—is called *Total Forgiveness*.[12] Wherever I preach it, it changes lives. I have a dream that I could preach this sermon to a million people of mixed race at the same time to see what would happen.

Those Christians who have manifested hate toward people who have a different color of skin are *unpopular in heaven*. They may not feel it. But mark it down, dear reader, the Lord Jesus feels it and will one day demonstrate it.

The attitude of many Christians regarding poverty.

God hates poverty. Proof of this is the way the poor are referred to throughout Scripture.

> "Because the poor are plundered, because the needy groan, I will now arise," says the LORD; "I will place him in the safety for which he longs."
>
> —PSALM 12:5, ESV

> All my bones shall say, "O LORD, who is like you, delivering the poor...and needy from him who robs him?"
>
> —PSALM 35:10, ESV

> Whoever is generous to the poor lends to the LORD, and he will repay him for his deed.
>
> —PROVERBS 19:17, ESV

> Whoever closes his ear to the cry of the poor will himself call out and not be answered.
>
> —PROVERBS 21:13, ESV

> Whoever oppresses the poor to increase his own wealth, or gives to the rich, will only come to poverty.
>
> —PROVERBS 22:16, ESV

> Whoever gives to the poor will not want, but he who hides his eyes will get many a curse.
>
> —PROVERBS 28:27, ESV

> Open your mouth, judge righteously, defend the rights of the poor and needy.
>
> —PROVERBS 31:9, ESV

Whatever differences Paul and James may have had, they agreed "to remember the poor" (Gal. 2:10). Some people have thought that James and Paul differed on the issue of justification by faith. James talks about justification by works. Martin Luther therefore disdained the Book of James, thinking James differed with Paul. Wrong. Had Luther seen the true meaning of James' view of works, he would never have disliked the Book of James. James' sole concern was the "poor man" (James 2:6, ESV) and has the poor man in mind in the rest of James chapter 2. Rather than having changed the subject, which many interpreters assume, James is *still* speaking of the poor man when he asks in verse 14, "Can faith save him?" (i.e., Can faith save the poor man?; ESV). He was not speaking of whether a person is saved or has assurance of salvation; he was referring to the *testimony* of the Christian and his or her effect on the poor man who needs to see that we care about him. Faith won't save the poor man out there; it is our good works that will make him want what we have. I deal with this in more detail in *Whatever Happened to the Gospel?*[13]

But sadly there was a preponderance of members of the Jerusalem church that was neglecting the poor, and James rebukes them. Not only that, but too many Christians have had the same attitude regarding the poor over the centuries. Indeed, genuine revival will result in a concern for the poor.

Terry Virgo describes five components of true revival:

1. A growing burden of prayer
2. An awakening of repentance among believers
3. A great hunger to hear preaching
4. A great conviction of sin leading to multiplied conversions
5. Distinct social change including a new awareness and care for the poor[14]

In other words, those who despise the poor are unpopular in heaven.

Gay marriage

I dealt with this already in chapter 3. You may recall that I stated a certain progression: rejection, acceptance, popularity. A prime example of this is the way gay marriage has come to be not only accepted but even popular.

Perhaps the greatest attack upon the God of the Bible is to undermine Him as our Creator. A distinction between the sexes is an example. It may begin with a seemingly innocent matter such as unisex hairdressers. It progresses to a demand of some to let males and females use the same restrooms in public places. The ultimate progression (so far) is to legitimize gay marriage. At the bottom is a hatred for the Creator God of the Bible.

When I wrote the book *Is God for the Homosexual?*[15] the idea of gay marriage was scarcely thought of with most people. I attempted to make the case that God *is indeed* for the homosexual. In fact the gay community largely applauded my book because they sensed a love and tenderness in me toward gay people. What they *didn't* like is my call for total abstinence. I stressed that heterosexual people must practice total abstinence until they are married. But the notion of gay people legitimizing their sleeping together by marriage was not a big issue when I wrote that book. My point is, the notion of gay marriage was not on most people's radar screen just thirty years ago. But now it is accepted, if not popular. Many people seem to regard it as cool nowadays, not realizing that they are a part of a devilish conspiracy to reject God as Creator, who made man "male and female" (Gen. 1:27).

It is a sad day when Christian ministers condone gay marriages. But that is how far the downward progression has come.

Sex outside of marriage

It is an assumption in Holy Scripture that a man and a woman will abstain from sleeping together until they are married. Joseph and Mary were engaged but did not sleep together. When the angel told Mary that she would give birth to a son she replied, "How will this be...since I am a virgin?" (Luke 1:34).

Surely every woman should make Mary their model and not give in to sleeping with a man until marriage. There is no way around this; it is a biblical assumption.

In the Old Testament if a man found out that the woman he married was not a virgin, she would be punished. She would be stoned (Deut. 22:20–21). At the very least, this demonstrates that, for women, the laws against sexual immorality included sex before marriage. That is not all; for if a man sleeps with a virgin before they are married, he was to pay a penalty of fifty shekels to her father *and* be required to marry her. "She shall be his wife, because he has violated her. He may not divorce her all his days" (Deut. 22:28–29, ESV).

It is not only common nowadays for non-Christian couples to sleep together without being married; it is common with many Christians. In many churches the pastor, church leader, or vicar never addresses the subject from the pulpit. It would seem that they are afraid of running off such couples. Some pastors fear losing the size of the congregations owing to this very issue.

Such pastors are unpopular in heaven. Those church leaders who condone sleeping together before marriage—or won't speak against it—are unpopular in heaven.

If the issue of whether you are popular in heaven or unpopular in heaven is important to you, I can assure you that the issues I have dealt with in this chapter are essential to your Christian life and reward at the judgment seat of Christ. For there you will give an account of "the things *done while in the body, whether good or bad*" (2 Cor. 5:10, emphasis added). There is time to change now. At the judgment seat of Christ it will be too late. I have written this book so that you will see the importance of being popular in heaven—where it matters. It is the only place that matters. Please, please wake up now! You will be so glad you took these words seriously.

Chapter 7

CAN WE KNOW WE ARE POPULAR IN HEAVEN?

Find out what pleases the Lord.

—Ephesians 5:10

When you are popular in heaven that means you are important in heaven. That is where being a VIP matters! Some want to be very important people below. But I want this book to make you desire to be a VIP among those in heaven. I really do mean it when I say I would prefer to be popular with the angels and the sainted dead—not to mention the persons of the Godhead—than to be popular here on earth.

So imagine this: being important in heaven. Wow. What a compliment! What an honor! Being important means having significance, having influence. What a privilege to have influence in heaven!

Am I to believe that we can have influence in heaven? Yes. After Jacob wrestled with an angel, he was not only given a name change (from Jacob to Israel) but was told:

> You have struggled with God and with humans and have overcome.
>
> —GENESIS 32:28

> As a prince hast thou power with God and with men, and hast prevailed.
>
> —GENESIS 32:28, KJV

> For you have striven with God and with men, and have prevailed.
>
> —GENESIS 32:28, ESV

Influence with God? Yes. The three Hebrews Shadrach, Meshach, and Abednego had so much influence in heaven for their refusal to bow down to the king's golden image that Jesus Himself got right into the burning fiery furnace with them (Dan. 3:25). I call that influence in heaven!

My time at Westminster Chapel was characterized by many life changes, including learning to dignify trials, practicing total forgiveness, showing gratitude, and learning how not to grieve the Holy Spirit. But there were two crisis moments that will bear mentioning at the beginning of this chapter. First, the decision to abandon my aspiration of becoming a world-class theologian and become an evangelist. Since the premise of my thesis at Oxford had met with rejection among some reformed theologians, I was determined to prove I had gotten it right regarding John Calvin (1509–1564) and the English Puritans, whom I nicknamed *experimental predestinarians* in my book *Calvin and English Calvinism to 1649*.[1] That became almost an obsession with me, I am ashamed to admit. But when Arthur Blessitt demonstrated how he talked to lost people out in the open in the streets of London, I was smitten from the crown of my head to the soles of my feet. I thought of these words from the great hymn "When I Saw the Cleansing Fountain," sometimes known as "I Will Praise Him":

Though the way seems straight and narrow,
All I claimed was swept away;
My ambitions, plans and wishes,
At my feet in ashes lay.

—Margaret J. Harris (1865–1919)

I died a thousand deaths that evening. I never looked back from that night when the Pilot Light ministry at Westminster Chapel was born. I was never to be the same again. But it was also humbling. Oh dear. No previous minister of the chapel would be seen in the streets of Victoria and Buckingham Palace passing out tracts and trying to get people saved. It was unprecedented. It was not helping my reputation as a Bible expositor. Although I did not have this phrase then, I knew that my decision was popular in heaven. But it was very unpopular with some of the middle-class members and deacons at Westminster Chapel.

The second crisis came during the year 2000 when I nervously began to contemplate life in America after we retired. We had decided to stay twenty-five years at Westminster. I gave the church fifteen months' notice. But what will I do when we return to the USA? I was barely known in America. I said to myself, "I will be fine. I will go out bone fishing twenty-four hours a day. I will become a recluse." It felt fairly good—until a voice clearly interrupted my thoughts: "Your ministry in America will be to Charismatics." "Oh no!" I thought. "Please!"

I don't know how this will make some readers feel, but I personally dislike being called a Charismatic. Besides, I wanted to reach Evangelicals. And the reformed Christians. I have the credentials, I know how they think, and I have what they need—an openness to the immediate and direct witness of the Holy Spirit. But no. Charismatics would be the pond in which I would fish. I was pretty sure then, and now am more sure, that was the Lord speaking to me. It did not bless me. But I have accepted it. I knew it would make me even more unpopular with Evangelicals. I'm sorry to be candid; I so wanted them to like me! But I knew I would be popular in heaven because I have embraced the stigma. God likes that. And, by the way, I have no complaints. The last sixteen years have worked out well. God has blessed us beyond measure; I have continued to write books and now preach all over the world.

These things said, if you make popularity in heaven your goal, you might as well forget being popular on earth—insofar as being popular *with the people you hoped to be popular with.* It comes to virtually the same thing as wanting to be popular when you were a teenager in school—as I pointed out in the beginning of this book.

This present chapter must be understood in terms of what is relative to the reader. What will be popular on earth to some would have no appeal whatever to someone else. But God knows our weaknesses; one man's meat is another man's misery. In my own situation I had to be willing to be looked down on by those people I had hoped to win over.

Protecting Your Reputation After You Die: Is This Good to Do?

One of the more disquieting things I have come across in my lifetime is how some people want to protect how they will be perceived after they die. If it is for the sake of truth as taught in Scripture, yes, they should want to preserve the *truth* that one taught so that it is not misunderstood or misused. But if they are trying to protect their *reputation* and good name, I am not sure this is the right way to go.

On my father's tombstone are these words: "A man of prayer." My stepmother, Abbie, to whom my dad was married for forty-eight years, came up with that very appropriate line regarding him. For that is what he was. But then I began to ask, "What do I want on my tombstone?" The more I think about it, I am not sure I want anything on my tombstone. It could be a way, possibly, of trying to control how I am perceived after I am gone. In any case this borders on trying to be popular on earth after I go to heaven. To put it another way, if I don't try to be popular on earth while I am alive, I certainly don't want to try to be popular on earth after I die. For after I am dead, the *only* thing that will matter to me then is whether or not I receive a "well done" from the lips of Jesus Himself.

I know one thing for sure: if my *goal* is to be popular on earth—whether it be getting the best invitations, selling more books, or having people say how good a person I am, I sadly forfeit the possibility of Jesus saying "well done" to me. I guarantee that.

Therefore, I want to make it my goal to be popular in heaven with the focus being what Jesus might say to me at the judgment seat of Christ.

The question is, "Can we know now that we are popular in heaven?" Yes, but we must be guarded. The twin sins of self-pity and self-righteousness are always lurking to creep inside our deceitful hearts. Never forget that, sadly, we never outgrow the heart being deceitful above all things and incurably wicked (Jer. 17:9). We therefore must not forget our propensity toward self-righteousness and self-pity when we attempt to assess whether we are popular in heaven. The greatest danger is to take ourselves too seriously. And yet we are aiming for something most valuable, most honoring to God, and therefore most important.

Ten Things That Please the Lord

It comes to this: finding out what pleases the Lord (Eph. 5:10). Paul would not have said this if it were not possible to come reasonably close to knowing whether we please the Lord. In chapter 4 I outlined what it means to seek after the praise that comes from God only. That is a quest that will most certainly lead you to please the Lord. I now list ten things—ten pursuits that I guarantee will cause you to be pleasing to the Lord. These are good indications that you are eschewing the praise of men and seeking after the honor that comes from God alone. There are, of course, more things I could mention, but I have chosen ten issues that will help us to know here on earth that we are popular in heaven.

1. Honoring the blood of Jesus

Satan hates the mention of the blood of Jesus, and here is why: it is what exposed his folly and sealed his downfall. The "accuser of our brothers" was "hurled down" (Rev. 12:10). Hence the message, "Woe to the earth and the sea, because the devil has gone down to you! He is filled with fury, because he knows that his time is short" (v. 12). Satan was hurled down—that is, consigned to hell, Tartarus, as we will see in some detail in the next chapter. As a consequence of this the blood of Jesus became our secret weapon to get the Father's immediate attention and defeat the devil. "They triumphed over him by the blood of the Lamb and by the word of their testimony; they did not love their lives so much as to shrink from death" (v. 11).

Satan orchestrated the crucifixion of Jesus. He actually thought the death of Jesus was his own idea. He had wanted to kill Jesus for a good while—any way he could (Luke 4:29; John 10:31–33). But eventually the devil entered Judas Iscariot (John 13:2). The chief priests, Herod, and Pontius Pilate were already on his side. From then on all went according to plan: the Jews and Romans killed Jesus at last by the cross. None of the princes of this world understood that this was actually God's own plan! Jesus was handed over to the authorities "by God's deliberate plan and foreknowledge" (Acts 2:23). Herod and Pilate did what God's power and will "decided beforehand should happen" (Acts 4:28). Isaiah saw the whole scenario in advance hundreds of years before: "The LORD has laid on him the iniquity of us all" (Isa. 53:6). The death of Jesus Christ on the cross was what was in God's mind from the foundation of the world (1 Pet. 1:19–20). The devil, the princes of this world—fallen angels, Herod, and Pilate—masterminded the crucifixion of Jesus, yes. But they did not have a clue what was actually going on, "for if they had, they would not have crucified the Lord of glory" (1 Cor. 2:8).

Some theologians take the view that the blood of Jesus means His death and may not necessarily refer to the actual *blood* that flowed from His head, side, hands, and feet. Therefore, some prefer to speak of "the cross" or His "death." They seem to want to eliminate speaking of the actual blood. They seem to think that to mention the literal blood is crude or crass. But I say that whereas referring to the cross may truly mean the blood of Christ, the New Testament writers emphasize the actual blood itself. They speak of the "sprinkled blood" (Heb. 12:24) and of being "sprinkled with his blood" (1 Pet. 1:2). Certainly the cross means His death (Gal. 6:14). But it is my view that particular attention to the actual blood that flowed from Jesus' body is essential to understanding why He had to die on the cross. It is the blood that is a "propitiation" for sin (Rom. 3:25, ESV); it turns the Father's wrath away. It satisfies His justice. Some people, however, don't apparently like to speak of Jesus' actual *blood* as it is possibly offensive to the sophisticated. But it is the very blood that flowed from Jesus' veins that is prefigured in the Old Testament and explicit in the New Testament. I will show three examples.

First, the blood that was sprinkled on the doorposts at Passover. It was one thing for lambs to be slaughtered; such prefigured the crucifixion of Jesus. But there was more: the Israelites were required by Moses, namely, "to take some of the blood and put it on the sides and tops of the doorframes of the houses where they eat the lambs" (Exod. 12:7).

> On that same night I will pass through Egypt and strike down every firstborn of both people and animals, and I will bring judgment on all the gods of Egypt. I am the Lord. The blood will be a sign for you on the houses where you are, and when I see the blood, I will pass over you.
>
> —Exodus 12:12–13

The word *blood* is stated two times: "the blood will be a sign for you," and "when I see the blood, I will pass over you." This foretold what would happen more than thirteen hundred years later. God saw His Son hanging on the cross. If you can picture the ancient doorposts silhouetted onto the cross—with the blood dripping from Jesus' head and hands—there you have it. God says, "When I see the blood, I will pass over your sins." Hallelujah!

Second, the ancient tabernacle in the wilderness prefigures the death of Christ. It shows a distinction between the slaughter of the animal on the altar and the actual blood that the high priest carried into the Most Holy Place. What is written in the Pentateuch (the first five books in the Old Testament) is a "shadow" of things to come (Heb. 10:1). The ancient priests took an animal and slaughtered it on the altar, which was out in the open. It was separate from the Most Holy Place. On the Day of Atonement the high priest took the very blood that came from the slaughtered animal and then sprinkled it on the mercy seat behind the curtain next to the Most Holy Place. The sacrificed lamb prefigured Jesus dying on the cross: Jesus dying out in the open. But His blood needed to be sprinkled on the Most Holy Place in heaven. It was in the Most Holy Place where atonement took effect. Jesus needed to enter heaven to sprinkle His blood on the heavenly mercy seat (Heb. 9:12).

Third, in the New Testament you have a further separation—in the Eucharist, the Lord's Supper. The bread refers to the body of

Jesus; the wine refers to His blood. The Lord's Supper is therefore in two parts—recognizing His body and also His blood:

> The Lord Jesus, on the night he was betrayed, took bread, and when he had given thanks, he broke it and said, "This is my body, which is for you; do this in remembrance of me." In the same way, after supper he took the cup, saying, "This cup is the new covenant in my blood; do this, whenever you drink it, in remembrance of me."
>
> —1 Corinthians 11:23–25

Jesus said we must eat His "flesh" *and* drink His "blood" (John 6:53–55). The Lord's Supper might have included only the bread since it symbolized Jesus' broken body. But separate recognition to Christ's *blood* is also a part of the liturgy. This is because God does not want us to be ashamed of His Son's shed blood.

The man I was named after, Dr. R.T. Williams, used to give this advice to ministers he ordained: "Honor the blood. And honor the Holy Ghost." That is a sure way of affirming the Word and the Spirit: honor the blood of Jesus and honor the Holy Spirit. Honoring the blood means not only to be unashamed of it, but actively and intentionally calling attention to that most precious blood. It is our secret weapon to get God's immediate attention and defeat the devil.

Don't be ashamed of the blood of Jesus. Honoring His blood will make you popular in heaven.

2. The willingness to go outside the camp

Jesus was crucified outside the gate of the city of Jerusalem. Why? The Jews crucifying Jesus outside the city continued an ancient practice of putting undesirable people outside the camp. It was sometimes a form of punishment. Whatever would be unclean was put outside the camp. "Outside the camp" was a nasty place. It was a place where people were sent for purification, but Jesus needed no purification; He was without sin (Heb. 4:15; 7:26). What He actually did outside the gate was to sanctify His people by His blood (Heb. 13:12).

Jerusalem was a walled city. If you entered or exited it, you went through a gate. Jesus was taken through one of those gates to be crucified outside the Holy City of Jerusalem. Jerusalem was too holy for a crucifixion to be allowed inside. Besides, Jesus was seen as a blasphemer, a criminal; such a horrible person should be put outside the Holy City in any case. A crucifixion inside the city was absolutely out of the question. The crucifixion outside the city gate was to denote further the unspeakable shame of this horrible man called Jesus. Hence He suffered "outside the city gate" (Heb. 13:12).

However, what Jesus was doing was very holy indeed. He suffered "to make the people holy through his own blood" (v. 12). We therefore honor what Jesus did for us by likewise going to Him "outside the city." It is a way of showing we are unashamed of the blood, the cross, and that we gladly identify with the disgrace He bore.

Yes. The glory of the Lord is outside the camp. If you truly seek the glory of God, begin your journey by going outside the camp. This may mean going outside the circle of your friends. It may mean going outside the company of the majority. It could in some cases mean going outside your denomination. It might mean going against the established leadership.

The glory of the Lord is outside the camp. Those who choose the glory of God over the praise that comes from people are popular in heaven. You may not be popular on earth. You may have to part from friends, relatives, and those who are held in high esteem—even your mentors.

Going outside the camp means to bear the stigma—the offense that inevitably comes from following the Lord closely. The word *stigma* is a pure Greek word that means offense. In the ancient

Hellenistic world the *stigma* was like a tattoo—a mark on runaway slaves. It was a reproach, a disgrace. In Acts 5:41 "the apostles left the Sanhedrin, rejoicing because they had been counted worthy of suffering disgrace for the Name." They willingly bore the stigma. Imagine that. Rejoicing for the privilege of being a shame in the sight of men!

I think the best word to denote stigma is *embarrassment*. When we bear the stigma it is embarrassing. But the apostles did not mind this. They rejoiced because they were "counted worthy"—a privilege from God! They were popular in heaven.

Outside the camp can be a lonely place. But you will be popular where popularity truly matters—in heaven. With God. With the angels. With those who accomplished great things by faith (Heb. 11), popularity with those who are in heaven now. They are the "great cloud of witnesses" (v. 1) who are rooting for you! They are for you! They are on your side! They are shouting, "Don't give up!" You don't hear them. Martin Luther on the night before he stood before the authorities at the Diet of Worms in 1521 cried out to God, "Are you dead? No, you cannot die; you only hide yourself." Luther felt nothing. But his willingness to go outside the camp changed the world.

Caution: what is outside the camp today often becomes tomorrow's camp. Those who initially go outside the camp sometimes become a new kind of majority later on—and become the camp of the next generation.

3. Going outside your comfort zone

We all by nature want to live within a comfort zone—whether temperature, what feels "at home," what we are familiar with, or where our friends are. The old wine always tastes better than new wine, said Jesus (Luke 5:39). We are comfortable with tradition, proven ways, what has been tested with time, and what makes us feel "good."

But what makes you and me feel "good" is not always what God has in mind for us. We may say that a certain preacher makes us "feel good." The sound of an old tune or song may cause us to "feel good." The scent of a flower, the aroma of our favorite food, the sound of a certain accent may give us a comfortable feeling. It is sometimes easy to confuse what makes us feel good with the real presence of God!

The ancient prophet Samuel was an example of "today's man" who had to yet again go outside his comfort zone. Having recognized that King Saul was "yesterday's man" even though Saul would reign another twenty years, Samuel was quickly told he had to find the next king—while Saul was very much alive. "The LORD said to Samuel, 'How long will you mourn for Saul, since I have rejected him as king over Israel? Fill your horn with oil and be on your way; I am sending you to Jesse of Bethlehem. I have chosen one of his sons to be king'" (1 Sam. 16:1). Samuel's immediate reaction was, "How can I go? If Saul hears about it, he will kill me" (v. 2).

How would you like the task of finding the next king when there is a reigning king who is utterly determined to stay put?

Despite being an old man and a legend in his own time, Samuel had to go outside his comfort zone. This had been Samuel's plight all his life! Now yet again he is required to go outside his comfort zone. God might have said to him, "Samuel, you have done well. You have done a good job for Me. I am proud of you. I want to reward you with a nice retirement. Go to a comfortable place and enjoy your final days in ease." No.

However old you are, however long you have been serving the Lord, however respected you might be, however many successes you have had, if you wish to maintain the anointing of the Holy Spirit, you have to go outside your comfort zone—again and again until God calls you home. The joy of being changed from "glory to glory" (2 Cor. 3:18, KJV) is granted to you on the condition you walk in the light (1 John 1:7) and maintain a willingness to go outside your comfort zone.

It hurts, yes. But popularity in heaven more than compensates for the pain of having to go outside your comfort zone. The items that now follow all have in common this matter of going outside your comfort zone. They are your guarantee of being popular in heaven.

4. Dignifying trials

To impute "pure joy" to a major trial is a challenging call to go outside your comfort zone. Our most natural reaction is to grumble. But listen to this: "Consider it pure joy, my brothers and sisters, whenever you face trials of many kinds" (James 1:2). This is the first statement that James—the half-brother of Jesus—makes at the beginning of his short epistle addressed to Jews everywhere. What a way to begin a letter!

The words "consider" (NIV) or "count" (KJV) come from the same Greek word Paul uses in his teaching of justification by faith alone: *elogisthe*—impute. God imputed righteousness to Abraham when Abraham believed the promise (Rom. 4:3). In the same way James is telling us to impute *joy* to the trial whenever that trial comes: "Consider it pure joy." In other words, regard the trial as something that is going to give you joy. Why? Because down the road you will see God was behind the trial! You will eventually be thankful for it, so be thankful for it now!

Why do you suppose James made this his first remark? It is because Jews who became Christians were undergoing all kinds of trials—persecution, dwindling numbers, quarrels within their fellowships, mistreatment from wealthier Christians, a tendency to disregard the poor and butter up the rich—which backfired on them. The Jerusalem church in particular—which probably influenced James to write this letter in the first place—was in a mess. They were not growing, and they had a sad lack of unity.

Near the beginning of my ministry at Westminster Chapel when I envisaged preaching through James many years ago, knowing that this verse about trials and temptations was right at the beginning, I somehow came up with a phrase "dignifying the trial." In other words, rather than showing contempt for a trial, treat it with grace and dignity. Instead of rejecting it, accept it. Treat the trial as a thing of beauty. Instead of denying it and sweeping it (so to speak) under the carpet, affirm it by welcoming it as a gift from God. I love the following verse from the hymn "Like a River Glorious":

> Every joy or trial falleth from above,
> Traced upon our dial by the Sun of Love;
> We may trust Him fully, all for us to do;
> They who trust Him wholly find Him wholly true.
>
> —Frances R. Havergal (1836–1879)

One way we dignify a trial is to let it run its course. Since it is designed by God in the first place, it will have both a beginning and an end. All trials come to an end. When we are in the middle of the trial we say, "Will this ever end?" "Will I ever get well?" "Will I ever come out of this?" But I can assure you, the trial will end.

Yes, every trial has a built-in time frame. It had a beginning, it will have an ending. During this time we can either dignify it or show contempt for it. We can try to make it end or let it run its course.

During that time, in my opinion, God is grading us. Yes. He watches us to see how we react to the trial He carefully designs for us. If we complain all through the trial, He writes, "Failed." If we dignify it, He writes, "Passed." You fail or pass. When you are angry with God and learn nothing from it, you fail. And God waits for another day to give us another chance. If you pass, God gives us an inner witness, "Well done," and we go to a higher degree of glory, as in 2 Corinthians 3:18.

For many years (I am ashamed to admit) I did the opposite of dignifying a trial. I would complain, battle through it, and when it finally subsided I only said, "Thank God that's over." God wrote "Failed" countless times. But when I came to see the value of a trial, I felt so ashamed and convicted. I reached the place I was determined to "pass" when a trial came so that God could elevate me to a higher level of grace.

At a critical moment in our early ministry, my wife, Louise, and I were faced with a most severe trial. I looked at her and said, "Either what I preach regarding dignifying trials is true or it isn't. I am determined to dignify this trial." We did. It was absolutely wonderful. The things we learned during that era were *so* good. *So* good.

I would urge you to do the same. Impute joy to your next trial or the one you are in right now. Here is a guarantee: the decision to dignify this trial will be popular in heaven. And God will catapult you to a higher level of knowing Him here on earth.

5. Showing gratitude

It is one thing to impute joy to a trial by not grumbling, it is quite another to maintain a lifestyle of thankfulness. Gratitude. Saying "thank You" to God for *every single thing* you should be thankful for. Every day. You may not feel thankful for a trial at first, but you can be thankful *in the trial* while it lasts. "Give thanks *in* all circumstances; for this is God's will for you in Christ Jesus" (1 Thess. 5:18, emphasis added).

But that is only the beginning. We need to develop a lifestyle of gratitude. That becomes the warp and woof of our daily lives.

I was given an amazing wake-up call by the Holy Spirit many years ago. In April 1986 I was preaching on Philippians 4:6:

> Do not be anxious about anything, but in every situation, by prayer and petition, with thanksgiving, present your requests to God.

This only happened to me once during my twenty-five years at Westminster Chapel. Right in the middle of my sermon, the Holy Spirit elbowed His way into my preaching. When I referred to the two words, "with thanksgiving," in that sermon, I was smitten all over—from the crown of my head to the soles of my feet and to the end of my fingertips. Never in my life had I felt anything like this. I felt horrible. As I spoke, my whole life came up before me. God showed me one thing after another for which I had not shown thankfulness. As I was preaching! Big things. The most salient things God had done for me, which I had not said "thank You" for. I felt so smitten in the middle of my sermon. I prayed as I preached, "Lord, help me to get this sermon over with so I can get to my vestry and pray."

Somehow I got through the sermon. I went into my vestry (pastor's office) and prayed and repented like I had not done in years. As I prayed, the Holy Spirit led me to see one thing after another I had not thanked God for. Huge things. The most obvious things.

"Lord, You *know* I'm thankful," I said to Him.

"But you didn't tell Me," He seemed to reply.

"But You *must* know I'm thankful for these things."

"You didn't tell Me."

The Lord continued to show me more things, dozens of things He had done for us but for which I had not taken the time to thank Him.

I did not realize that saying thank You meant so much to Him! I assumed that He would know my mind and clearly see that I was very thankful—delivering me from severe trials in London, looking after my family, giving to me Louise, my children, T. R. and Melissa, His putting me in Westminster Chapel, finishing well at Oxford (it wasn't easy), giving me deacons who loved me, giving me a writing ministry. It went on and on.

I made a vow that day—on November 13, 1988—to be a thankful man. It is a vow I have kept. I keep a journal. I write in it daily so that I do not forget any event. I could tell you where I was at 3:00 p.m. April 6, 1984, or July 26, 1992. So here is what I vowed to do in my vestry that Sunday morning: to go through my journal every morning and thank God for every single item of the previous day for which I should be thankful. It takes about twenty seconds! God wants us to say thank You.

Here is what I have learned: gratitude is very, very important to God. I had not realized this. Take for example the time Jesus healed ten lepers. Yes, ten were healed but only one came back to thank Jesus. His immediate reaction was, "Where are the other nine?" (Luke 17:17). I have concluded three things from this:

1. God loves gratitude. It honors Him.
2. God hates ingratitude. He notices when we fail to say thank You.
3. Gratitude must be taught. I began teaching it from that time.

The doctrine of sanctification is essentially the doctrine of gratitude. Sanctification is not what saves us; sanctification—living a holy life—is saying thank You to God. If sanctification saves us, then salvation is by works. But salvation is by grace through faith alone (Eph. 2:8–9). So why live a godly life? As Dr. D. James Kennedy used to put it: it is like a PS at the end of a letter when we say, "Thank You, Lord, for saving my soul."

But it must be taught. God hates ingratitude. So do you! When you do someone a big favor and they don't bother to say thank you, does it not irk you? When they say thank you, you may say,

"Don't mention it." But *woe unto them* if they don't mention it! Of course you want them to appreciate what you did for them.

God is a jealous God. Part of that jealousy is that He wants to govern our lives, and He wants us to be thankful for what He does for us. In Romans 1 when Paul lists sins of debauchery and all that angers God, we have near the beginning of the list: "Although they knew God, they neither glorified him as God *nor gave thanks to him*" (v. 21, emphasis added). In the last days, said Paul, people would be "ungrateful" (2 Tim. 3:2). Indeed, the curse of our age is a feeling of entitlement. Instead of being thankful people are angry for not getting their rights. They transfer this feeling of entitlement to God and are angry with Him because He does not bow down to them. The truth is, we are a people of ingratitude.

By the way, here is a fringe benefit of being thankful. Medical people have been saying that thankful people live longer! Psychologists have said it; doctors of medicine are saying it![2]

God owes us nothing. That may be a hard pill to swallow. But it's the truth. Therefore, when God shows kindness to us whether by giving us good health or answering our prayers, we should be *careful to remember* to say thank You. For further reading see my book *Just Say Thanks*.[3]

Do you want to be popular in heaven? Be a thankful person. Thank God for every single thing He does for you. Suggestion: think of at least three things a day to thank Him for before you go to bed each night; heaven is watching.

One last thing: an old friend used to say to me, "God cannot stand praise." What he meant was, God blesses you back! You cannot out-give the Lord, neither can you out-thank the Lord!

6. Generosity

"God loves a cheerful giver" (2 Cor. 9:7). John Wesley (1703–1791) said that the last part of a person to be converted is their wallet. The French atheist Voltaire (1694–1778) said that when it comes to money, every person's religion is the same. We say in Kentucky, "When a feller says, 'It ain't the money, it's the principle'; it's the money."

In 1983 I wrote a book called *Tithing*. It is still in print in several languages. It is endorsed by Billy Graham and the Archbishop of Canterbury. Tithing did not begin with the Mosaic Law; it began with Abraham, four hundred years before the Law came (Gen. 14). When Jesus died on the cross, the Law was perfectly fulfilled (Col. 2:14). It takes us back to Abraham, the prototype Christian. This means the gospel first preached to Abraham (Gal. 3:8) is our gospel. Abraham was Paul's exhibit A for his teaching of justification by faith alone (Rom. 4). We take also our cue from Abraham, who was the first tither. How did he know to give God one-tenth? It was revealed to him by the Holy Spirit; it was the biblical way by which the gospel would be supported. The Law came in four hundred years later and made it mandatory—you were required to do it. Abraham was not required to tithe; he chose to. That is the biblical principle to this day: tithing is a choice. And yet its validity was affirmed by Jesus (Matt. 23:23) and assumed by Paul. When Paul said the Christian should give "in keeping with your income" (1 Cor. 16:2), he merely continued the tithing principle. And yet we do it out of gratitude to God.

Tithing is the minimum. It is the beginning. Under the Law, not to tithe was to "rob" God (Mal. 3:8). We have every reason to conclude the same thing even though we are not under the Law. The tithe belongs to God (Lev. 27:30); we are on our honor to give to Him what is His. Those who don't do this still rob God. The tithing principle that began with Abraham is to be continued by you and me. Those who don't tithe do not realize that they rob God and are impoverished. They don't realize the blessing that would be theirs if they began to tithe—and kept it up.

What is fascinating is that even under the Law they were promised blessing if they gave God what is His. Amazing. God did not need to motivate them like that. He graciously stooped to their weakness to encourage them to do the right thing. How much more is that true with us who are not under the Law! "See if I will not throw open the floodgates of heaven and pour out so much blessing that there will not be room enough to store it" (Mal. 3:10).

Funny thing, this. The Bible never once attempts to prove God's existence. The theologians try to do this. God Himself doesn't. However, the nearest He comes to proving His existence is by tithing. "Prove me" (Mal. 3:10, KJV), says the Lord, and find out how real God is! Paul put it like this: "Whoever sows sparingly will also reap sparingly, and whoever sows generously will also reap generously" (2 Cor. 9:6).

My father taught me to tithe. He held to what you might call a mathematical incredulity. He always said that if we give to God what is His, that the 90 percent we live on will *go as far* as the 100 percent we have from the start. And he would add, "Son, sometimes I think the money goes even further." My dad was not a wealthy man. But he always had enough. More than enough.

But heaven is not pleased with the person who gives grudgingly or resentfully. This is because "God loves a cheerful giver" (2 Cor. 9:7). The word *cheerful* comes from the Greek word *hilaros,* from which we get the word *hilarious.* Some interpreters argue therefore that Paul means God loves a hilarious giver!

I know this as much as I know anything in the world. God honors generosity. Generosity will make you popular in heaven. God will show you on earth that you cannot out-give Him. Don't expect this to happen on the first day! But over the years you will see it: you cannot out-give the Lord. It is His nature to show He is pleased with you.

Generosity is one more way you can know you are popular in heaven. That is, unless you are self-righteous about it. If you give for everybody to see, you forfeit popularity in heaven and settle for a lesser reward—being popular on earth. That is being like a Pharisee; all they did was for people to see (Matt. 23:5). Jesus said we must not let our left hand know what our right hand does when it comes to giving (Matt. 6:3). In other words, there is a sense in which we don't even tell ourselves when we are generous.

You therefore make a choice: to be popular in heaven or be popular in the here and now.

7. Graciousness

In Philippians 4:5 Paul says, "Let your gentleness be evident to all." The New Living Translation says, "Let everyone see that you are considerate in all you do." The King James Version translates the Greek word *epieikes* as "moderation." The English Standard Version uses "reasonableness." The Amplified Version offers several possible translations: "graciousness, unselfishness, mercy, tolerance, and patience."

The background of the Greek word *epieikes* is this: you have discovered that your enemy is clearly in the wrong, and you have caught them red-handed; their wrongdoing is out in the open and there is no doubt of their being in the wrong. But you let them off the hook instead of pointing the finger or accusing them. You could say, "Gotcha," and throw the book at them. But no. Instead you overlook it. You let them save face.

The best English word for the Greek *epieikes* is *graciousness*. Proverbs 19:11 tells us that "a person's wisdom yields patience; it is to one's glory to overlook an offense." The translation of this proverb from Spanish is, "It is his glory to rise above an offense."[4]

This is hard to do! But it will make you popular in heaven.

The next time you have caught someone to be unquestionably in the wrong, what do you do? It could be an enemy. Your wife. Your husband. The person who has been out to get you is found guilty. What do you do? Do you throw the book at them? After all, they have been caught. Found out. Clearly guilty. No doubt about it.

Graciousness would be to drop it. Look the other way. Refuse to accuse or get even. Never mention it. Never look back. Let them go. Set them free. Wow. And then you tell no one you did it! Why? Because you want to be popular in heaven.

I was preaching in Northern Ireland when a pastor said to me, "I love your book on unhappy marriage." I said to him, "I have not written a book on unhappy marriage." "Oh yes you have," he insisted; "it changed my life." Then I realized he was speaking of my book *The Thorn in the Flesh,* in which there is a single chapter called "An Unhappy Marriage." He then asked me: "Can your wife be your enemy?" I smiled and said, "Yes." It seemed to have made his day!

Graciousness then would be to let your husband, your wife, your enemy—anyone who is openly found out—*off the hook.* It takes great grace to do this. But that is the way God is to us (Ps. 103:12). And when *we* are that way, this being true godliness, we are popular in heaven.

8. Total Forgiveness

This is actually taking graciousness a step further, filling out all the implications of what it means to forgive—but doing it *totally*. It is totally forgiving others. It is also totally forgiving yourself. It is totally letting God off the hook for what He has for some reason allowed to happen to you. I would have thought total forgiveness is the hardest thing in the world to carry out and keep doing it. The most natural thing in the world is to want vengeance on the person who has wronged you. You want them to get their comeuppance—to get what should be coming to them. Sheer punishment and pain for what they did to you. I sympathize. I've been there. But an old friend Josef Tson said to me in our darkest hour: "R. T., you must totally forgive them. Until you totally have forgiven them, you will be in chains. Release them, and you will be released."

Total forgiveness is like climbing Mount Everest. Few people do it. It is however an achievable goal. It comes by an act of the will. God will not knock you down to cause you to do it; He merely puts the option to you. Then you make a choice, and that choice ultimately comes to this: to be popular in heaven or get vengeance here below.

Total forgiveness is not approving of what they did to you. Jesus said to the woman found in adultery: "Neither do I condemn you.... Go now and leave your life of sin" (John 8:11). Nor is total forgiveness to live in denial, refusing to admit that what they did was horrible. Some people have been so hurt that it is easier to deny what they did than to face the pain. Total forgiveness is consciously admitting to what they did and also setting them free. You need to *realize* they were horrible. Admit it. What will make you popular in heaven is not living in denial but consciously coming to terms with their wrongdoing—and then letting them off the hook.

It means not telling anybody what they did to you unless it was a crime. A crime must be reported. But the real reason we tell what they did is to keep people from admiring them. You naturally want to hurt their reputation, but this is unacceptable. You can certainly tell *one* other person for therapeutic reasons. And you can pour your complaint out to God (Ps. 142:2). He welcomes this. But hide their horrible injustice from others, as God has forgiven you (Eph. 4:32). Don't let them be afraid of you; don't let them feel intimidated by you. Be gracious instead. Don't let them feel guilty; it is God's job to make them see their wrong. Let them save face. Instead of rubbing their noses in it, give them a way out so they even feel good about what they did—as Joseph did to his brothers (Gen. 45:5–8).

Don't go to them and say, "I forgive you for what you did." This is your way of trying to let them know how hurt you are, even if you are not aware of your motives. Hide from them that you have forgiven them. Tell God. Nine out of ten people we have to forgive don't think they have done anything wrong anyway! The *only* time you say, "I forgive you," is when they are asking for it. That is different; you must set them free then. But what gets our goat is that they don't know how deeply offended we are. Just tell God.

Protect them from their darkest secret. Chances are you know something about someone that could destroy them. Assure them that you will *never* reveal it. Not only that, total forgiveness is a commitment for life. Your physician may tell you, "This tablet is a life sentence; you must take it all your life." So too forgiving totally. You have to do it today. Tomorrow. A year from now. Ten years from now. Don't expect them to come around because you have been praying for them. They don't know this and are not to know this. This is what makes you popular in heaven!

And, yes, total forgiveness means that *you pray for them.* You don't say, "Lord, I commit them to You" (when you say that, you possibly hope God will bring vengeance on them). You ask God to *bless* them. You pray this from your heart, literally asking God to bless them. Yes, it is the hardest thing in the world to do. But popularity in heaven is worth it! "Great is your reward in heaven" (Matt. 5:12). Bless those that curse you: "Love your enemies, do good to those who hate you.... *Then your reward will be great, and you will be children of the Most High, because he is kind to the ungrateful and wicked*" (Luke 6:27, 35, emphasis added).

What is the great reward? Popularity in heaven—for a start. Who knows what else God might do to reward you? If it is a "well done" from Jesus, that is good enough for me! For further study see my trilogy *Total Forgiveness, How to Forgive Ourselves—Totally,* and *Totally Forgiving God.*

9. Letting God vindicate you

Vindication means being cleared from blame or suspicion. For many years the desire for vindication was my uppermost wish. I can't say I have completely outgrown this desire, but it has not been as important to me as it once was. But when you know there are people out there who believe what is untrue, it would be nice if your name was cleared. But I have learned to take the withholding of vindication to be for my good. More than that, I have learned that God has a way of vindicating that far exceeds what I might have wanted!

God is the expert vindicator. Here is the inflexible rule: don't deprive Him of getting to do what He delights in doing and what He does best. Vindicating is what He does. You find it no fewer than three times in Scripture: "It is mine to avenge; I will repay" (Deut. 32:35; Rom. 12:19; Heb. 10:30).

The most important thing to remember about vindication is that God only vindicates the *truth*. It is not that He is not interested in *you*. But it is the truth that matters. In other words, if you have been true and honest, if you have upheld the truth, that is what matters to God! To put it another way, if you have vindication coming because the truth is at stake, then vindication will be your inheritance. Count on it.

But don't try to make it happen! God doesn't like that. At all! Keep your hands off the situation and step back. Watch Him work. Let Him do it. But the moment you say to yourself, "I must make this easy for God. I will step in and do His work for Him," God will back off and turn it over to you. It is as if He says, "Go on—you do it." And what follows is things get worse than ever! *Don't do His work for Him.* Like justification by faith alone, He gets all the glory. If you try to add works to your faith to ensure you are saved, you risk forfeiting saving faith. God does not want your help in justification; it is what He does. Your faith alone justifies. Your faith alone sets Him free to do what He delights to do.

Caution: vindication may not come soon. I mentioned above our being in a severe trial at Westminster Chapel. I had been there for six years. False charges were thrown at me by some of the deacons—all good men. Their credibility was scary; they were solid, God-honoring men. All of them are in heaven now. But they wanted to get rid of me. I understood how they felt. But I longed for God to step in! I remember reading in 2 Thessalonians 1:6–7: "God is just: He will pay back trouble to those who trouble you and give relief to you who are troubled." "Oh good," I thought. "Wow. Wonderful." But then I had to keep reading: "This will happen when the Lord Jesus is revealed from heaven in blazing fire with his powerful angels" (v. 7). Oh dear. That meant waiting a long time.

Sometimes God does step in, however, in this life. The greatest wish for vindication I ever had was for God to make my own father see the truth. In 1956 he said to me, "Son, you have broken with God. You have recanted on holiness." That hurt a lot. It was not true. But he sincerely believed this because I had changed my view of sanctification. I had been brought up to believe that we could be sinless! Verses such as 1 John 1:8, "If we claim to be without sin, we deceive ourselves and the truth is not in us," made me see how wrong my theological upbringing at this point was. I also wondered, "Why would Jesus give us the Lord's Prayer in which there is a petition that we should ask God to forgive our sins, debts, or trespasses if we could reach a state in which we never sin (Matt. 6:12; Luke 11:4)? I wanted so much for him to see that I was following the Lord. I told him that he would see the truth in one year. But a year later I was out of the ministry. Five years later I was selling vacuum cleaners door to door. My dad felt totally vindicated in his view about me. But many years later when he came to see me at Westminster Chapel, he said to me: "Son, I am proud of you. You were right, I was wrong." I was glad to hear that of course, but the truth is, by then it did not mean that much to me after all.

I think that sometimes God withholds vindication from us to

keep us on our knees, seeking His face, and so it won't mean so much to us.

Vindication is God's enterprise. That's His turf. It is what He does. Let Him do it. This pleases Him, and you will be popular in heaven. Even if He chooses to withhold vindication from you.

10. Not grieving the Holy Spirit

Last on my list, but certainly not the least important, is my understanding regarding the "ways" of the Holy Spirit. It is possibly the insight I cherish most in my entire ministry. In my own life this insight preceded my coming into total forgiveness. It prepared me for it. I had learned to cherish not grieving the Spirit so that when Josef Tson said to me, "You must totally forgive them," I took this with both hands. This teaching is guaranteed to change your life if you will be determined to keep from grieving the Holy Spirit. There are two relevant passages.

> Then John gave this testimony: "I saw the Spirit come down from heaven as a dove and remain on him [Jesus]. And I myself did not know him, but the one who sent me to baptize with water told me, 'The man on whom you see the Spirit come down and remain is the one who will baptize with the Holy Spirit.' I have seen and I testify that this is God's Chosen One."
>
> —John 1:32–34

> And do not grieve the Holy Spirit of God, with whom you were sealed for the day of redemption. Get rid of all bitterness, rage and anger, brawling and slander, along with every form of malice. Be kind and compassionate to one another, forgiving each other, just as in Christ God forgave you.
>
> —Ephesians 4:30–32

The Holy Spirit is a person, a very, very sensitive person. When we speak of a person being "hypersensitive" it is certainly not a compliment. But like it or not, that is the way the Holy Spirit is. This may surprise you, but grieving the Holy Spirit is probably the easiest thing in the world to do. You do it when you don't realize you are doing it. When you are angry, you grieve the Spirit. When you lose your temper, you grieve the Spirit. When you speak of another person so as to make that person look bad, you grieve the Spirit. When you are unkind, you grieve the Spirit. And if you do not totally forgive as God forgave you, you grieve the Holy Spirit.

The word *grieve* is from the Greek *lupeo.* It can mean getting your feelings hurt. The Holy Spirit is depicted in the New Testament as a dove. You possibly knew that already, but did you notice the word *remain* in the passage above, John 1:32–34? It is there twice; the Holy Spirit came down on Jesus and remained. It is my own experience, sadly, that when the Holy Spirit comes down on me, He doesn't stay for long. Mind you, I am using a metaphor, for the Holy Spirit never leaves us (John 14:16). But when, as it were, the Dove "lifts" rather than remaining, we lose the *sense* of His presence. But when the Dove came down on Jesus, He stayed. He never left. He felt at home! Jesus never, ever grieved the Holy Spirit.

You probably also know that doves and pigeons are in the same family. Anatomically they are identical. But temperamentally they are vastly different. You can train a pigeon; you cannot train a dove. Pigeons are boisterous; doves are gentle. In my book *Pigeon Religion* I show nineteen differences between doves and pigeons and how their behavior can be transferred to how we live the Christian life.

When the Holy Spirit is in us *ungrieved,* we feel the liberty that comes from Him. Love. Joy. Peace. All the fruit of the Holy Spirit (Gal. 5:22–23). The ungrieved Spirit in us grants us clear thinking. Insight. It is how I prepare sermons and write books. Without the ungrieved Spirit I am finished. Done.

This is a further reason for being popular in heaven. When I lose my temper, point the finger, hold a grudge, keep a record of wrongs (1 Cor. 13:5), or speak evil of someone, the Dove lifts, as it were—and I am not even able to prepare a sermon! I am left to my own intellect. It means no fresh insight, only what others have said for centuries. That is not the way I want to function.

When Paul said, "Find out what pleases the Lord" (Eph. 5:10), he had just cautioned against grieving the Spirit. Bitterness and holding grudges is not the only way to grieve the Spirit; so too does sexual immorality and greed (vv. 1–7). To be popular in heaven, then, means living a godly life, both inwardly, when we are devoid of bitterness, and outwardly, when we are sexually pure and squeaky-clean when it comes to money issues.

Popularity in heaven, then, costs. It is the equivalent of wisdom that begins with the fear of the Lord (Prov. 1:7).

> The beginning of wisdom is this: Get wisdom.
> Though it cost you all you have, get understanding.
> Cherish her, and she will exalt you;
> embrace her, and she will honor you.
> She will give you a garland to grace your head
> and present you with a glorious crown.
>
> —Proverbs 4:7–9

It comes to those who make a choice—whether to soak in the praise that comes from people or to seek after the praise that comes from God (John 5:44). All I have written in this chapter is merely an unfolding of how John 5:44 is applied. It is guaranteed to make you popular in heaven.

You can know it now. The Spirit will witness this to you as long as you don't begin to take yourself too seriously. For we never graduate from the deceitful heart, which remains desperately wicked (Jer. 17:9). For I also guarantee that the moment you begin to feel a little bit comfortable in yourself and fancy that you have "arrived," God will bring you down so fast that you won't know what hit you. You must take His gracious smile—a witness that you are popular in heaven—with deepest humility.

"It ain't over till it's over." Refuse to let your left hand know what your right hand is doing—whether in generosity or graciousness. Until the day arrives and Jesus says to you, "Well done."

None of us are there yet.

PART II

FAMOUS IN HELL

Jesus I know, and Paul I know about, but who are you?

—Acts 19:15

Chapter 8

THE WORLD OF TARTARUS

God did not spare angels when they sinned,
but sent them to hell [Tartarus].

—2 Peter 2:4

I am not an expert in demonology, nor do I want to be. It is my own pastoral experience that people who are fascinated with demons are, so it seems to me, usually not very spiritual, but have an eerie curiosity that reflects a spiritual immaturity. I have never chosen to preach on this subject in my entire ministry and do so only when the text calls for it in a series, on a particular book, or when I have been specifically asked to speak on it.

I recall doing a series of talks on spiritual warfare at the London City Mission many years ago, but it is never a subject I would have chosen. I vividly recall that at Westminster Chapel the text required that I deal with the subject of the demonic over two Sunday evenings. I remember so well how I experienced unusual opposition and warfare during those two weeks that was not of this earth. I also remember how the strangest people turned up in the services. Incredible. Bizarre. We suffered no harm from any of this, but I have to say I did not enjoy those two weeks.

There are two extremes that must be avoided. Satan would love to get us in either of these traps.

1. Focus on the demonic all the time
2. Never to deal with it at all

Concerning the latter, Satan would prefer you to believe that he does not exist. To deal with this kind of subject shows how real he is. But he equally loves it if we talk about him all the time and get people preoccupied with things of the demonic world. I had a church member in Lower Heyford, England, who was proud of his shelf full of books about the devil and stories of demon possession. But he came to church very irregularly and did not appear to be the slightest bit interested in solid theology.

There are some very important principles we learn from Jude and Peter. These two New Testament writers refer to the ancient Gnostics, who were among the first ancient enemies of the early church. The Gnostics were interlopers, intruders who infiltrated the early church. They came in through the back door (Jude 4). They denied that Jesus Christ has come in the flesh (1 John 4:1–3). The word *gnostic* comes from the Greek *gnosis* (knowledge). These men promised a new way of knowing; they claimed that they could make the Christian faith better by their input. The truth is, they were utter enemies of the faith of Jesus Christ. Their aim was to destroy the church of Jesus Christ. As we will see below, they were popular in hell.

They also showed themselves to be fools when it comes to confronting the demonic. The expression "fools rush in where angels fear to tread," as Alexander Pope (1688–1744) put it,[1] was derived from Jude and Peter. These two writers caution us that we must show simultaneous *respect* and *contempt* when it comes to confronting the authorities and powers in Tartarus. The Gnostics "reject authority and heap abuse on celestial beings" (Jude 8). They "slander whatever they do not understand" (v. 10). "Bold and arrogant, they are not afraid to heap abuse on celestial beings" (2 Pet. 2:10). Peter and Jude show how God's own angels deal with those who inhabit the world of Tartarus:

> Even angels, although they are stronger and more powerful, do not heap abuse on such beings when bringing judgment on them from the Lord. But these people blaspheme in matters they do not understand.
>
> —2 PETER 2:11–12

Note how Peter put it: "Even angels"! Angels are more powerful than demons. But even angels don't play games with the evil spirits. And yet there is more:

> Even the archangel Michael, when he was disputing with the devil about the body of Moses, did not himself dare to condemn him for slander but said, "The Lord rebuke you!"
>
> —JUDE 9

We learn two things from this: first, do not rebuke Satan directly on your own. Say, "The Lord rebuke you." The Lord does not give us power to rebuke Satan but rather to resist him. If you say, "But Jesus rebuked Satan," I reply: you are not Jesus. Not only that, Zechariah 3:2 tells us specifically that it is the Lord who rebukes Satan: "The LORD said to Satan, 'The LORD rebuke you, Satan!'" Second, as I said, we learn to show simultaneous *respect* and *contempt* for the demonic.

I have been surprised over the years to see how many Christians are so quick to say, "I rebuke you, Satan"—or words to that effect. You are rushing into where angels fear to tread. Remember that even Michael the archangel did not address the devil like that! He said, "The Lord rebuke you" (Jude 9).

These things said, one should not be afraid of the devil. He is second to God in power and wisdom—yes. But a far second! He is pitifully weak compared to almighty God. Do not be like some who have more fear of the devil than they do of God!

You do not need to be afraid of the devil. A healthy awareness of his being around is essential, yes. Paul said, "We are not unaware of his schemes" (2 Cor. 2:11). Satan shows up in at least two ways you should know about: openly, when he ends up overreaching himself, or covertly, when he "masquerades as an angel of light" (2 Cor. 11:14). Above all remember that he is resistible. If you resist him, he will be seen to have overreached himself. The prime example of how Satan overreaches himself was that he masterminded the crucifixion of Jesus. But it was his downfall. He had no idea what God was up to. "None of the rulers of this age understood it, for if they had, they would not have crucified the Lord of glory" (1 Cor. 2:8). That is one of the reasons the devil is threatened by mention of the blood of Jesus Christ. Get to know God's ways and the unique ways of the Holy Spirit. Greater is He that is in you than he that is in the world (1 John 4:4).

> Be alert and of sober mind. Your enemy the devil prowls around like a roaring lion looking for someone to devour. Resist him, standing firm in the faith, because you know that the family of believers throughout the world is undergoing the same kind of sufferings.
>
> —1 Peter 5:8–9

> Resist the devil, and he will flee from you.
>
> —James 4:7

Yes, you should know these verses in Scripture that show that the devil exists and that he is your enemy not your friend. But don't try to be an expert on the devil. Being aware of his devices, as I am showing you, is certainly enough. Moreover, Martin Luther (1483–1546) used to say that the one thing the devil cannot stand is ridicule. I love the verse in Luther's hymn "A Mighty Fortress Is Our God":

> And though this world, with devils filled, should threaten
> to undo us,
> We will not fear, for God hath willed His truth to triumph
> through us;
> The Prince of Darkness grim, we tremble not for him;
> His rage we can endure, for lo, his doom is sure,
> One little word shall fell him.

We don't know as much as we may like to regarding the origin and fall of Satan. You may be sure that God has told us all we need to know. Here is what we may rightly assume: Satan was created by God. Indeed, he was created by Jesus Christ. This of course refers to the way Satan was created *before his revolt*—not afterward.

> For by him [Christ] all things were created: things in heaven and on earth, visible and invisible, whether thrones or powers or rulers or authorities; all things have been created through him and for him. He is before all things, and in him all things hold together.
>
> —Colossians 1:16–17

It seems likely that Isaiah was given an insight regarding Satan—known as "Lucifer, son of the morning" (Isa. 14:12, KJV) or "Day Star, son of Dawn" (ESV). This seems to be the way Satan was identified before his revolt against the Most High.

> How you are fallen from heaven,
> morning star, son of the dawn!
> You have been cast down to the earth,
> you who once laid low the nations!
> You said in your heart,
> "I will ascend to the heavens;
> I will raise my throne
> above the stars of God;
> I will sit enthroned on the mount of assembly,
> on the utmost heights of Mount Zaphon.
> I will ascend above the tops of the clouds;
> I will make myself like the Most High."
>
> —Isaiah 14:12–14

So it is clear that there was a revolt in heaven before the fall of man in the Garden of Eden. How long before the fall did this revolt take place? Who knows? Here is what we know for sure: Satan was created by God. Satan is therefore not eternal, that is, he did not exist in eternity alongside God; Satan is a creation of God. Jude tells us that the angels "who did not keep their positions of authority but abandoned their proper dwelling—these he has kept in darkness, bound with everlasting chains for judgment on the great Day" (Jude 6). This parallels 2 Peter 2:4, quoted at the beginning of this chapter. It is also possible that Satan took a third of the angels with him, if that is what Revelation 12:4 is referring to. These angels lost their place in heaven. Satan was "hurled to the earth, and his angels with him" (v. 9).

According to 2 Peter 2:4 these angels were sent to hell, or Tartarus. It is this word that we have in mind when I speak of "famous in hell." There are three Greek words that are translated *hell* in many versions.

1. *Gehenna*, used twelve times in the New Testament, originally refers to the rubbish dump that burned continually outside Jerusalem. It is often connected to fire. In other words, hellfire comes from *Gehenna*. That is *not* what we mean in this book by famous in hell.

2. There is *Hades*. Used twelve times in the Greek New Testament, *Hades* literally means the grave or death. However, some translators have used it in certain verses as a synonym for *hell*, as in Matthew 16:18 when Jesus said to Peter, "The gates of Hades [hell] shall not prevail against it," and in Luke 16:23, "In Hades [hell], where he was in torment, he looked up and saw Abraham far away." In any case, hades is *not* what this book means by being famous in hell.

3. In Greek mythology Tartarus is the deep abyss that is used as a dungeon of torment and suffering for the wicked and as a prison for the Titans. It was regarded as a place in the underworld, even lower than *Hades*. In Roman mythology it is the place where the enemies of the gods are sent.

   Used only once in the New Testament as the verb *tartaroo,* "to thrust down to Tartarus...to hold captive in Tartarus."[2]

God did not spare angels when they sinned, but sent them to hell, putting them in chains of darkness to be held for judgment.

—2 Peter 2:4

> God did not spare angels when they sinned, but cast them into hell and committed them to chains of gloomy darkness to be kept until the judgment.
>
> —2 Peter 2:4, esv

As just seen above, Jude was referring to Tartarus:

> And the angels who did not stay within their own position of authority, but left their proper dwelling, he has kept in eternal chains under gloomy darkness until the judgment of the great day.
>
> —Jude 6, esv

Writing under the infallible inspiration of the Holy Spirit, then, Peter and Jude assume its existence even though it was a part of both Roman and Greek mythology. *It is where the fallen angels are now.* The fallen angels—evil spirits, or demons—are in a pre-judgment existence. It is a conscious existence. Though they are in chains, they are given limited liberty and are at enmity with Jesus Christ and those united to Him. They lurk about in the world. Their aim is to destroy the works of God. They seek to thwart the purpose of God. They oppress and possess. Demon possession is best understood as evil spirits of Tartarus who somehow get into some of the minds of human beings. They await final judgment. They know their final destiny. They cried out to Jesus, "Have you come here to torment us before the time?" (Matt. 8:29, esv). This indicates that they know their end. Satan "knows that his time is short" (Rev. 12:12). By the way, the next time the devil reminds you of your past, remind him of his future!

Therefore, when the seven sons of Sceva thought that casting out demons was a new kind of game, they overreached themselves. Here is the biblical account:

> Then some of the itinerant Jewish exorcists undertook to invoke the name of the Lord Jesus over those who had evil spirits, saying, "I adjure you by the Jesus whom Paul proclaims." Seven sons of a Jewish high priest named Sceva were doing this. But the evil spirit answered them, "Jesus I know, and Paul I recognize, but who are you?" And the man in whom was the evil spirit leaped on them, mastered all of them and overpowered them, so that they fled out of that house naked and wounded.
>
> —Acts 19:13–16, esv

Demon possession, as we will see further in the next chapter, is a no-joke thing.

Chapter 9

SEVEN FACTS REGARDING DEMON POSSESSION

Test everything; hold fast what is good.

—1 Thessalonians 5:21, esv

Casting out demons is not a game. It is not fun. It is serious, serious business. In this chapter I want to unfold seven fundamental truths—facts—regarding the demonic that one should be aware of.

1. Demon Possession Is Real

Make no mistake, evil spirits possess some people. The devil would prefer that you believe that he does not exist at all. But if some demand proof, look no further than seeing a person possessed by the devil.

That said, there is a difference between demon possession and demon oppression, although it is not so easy to explain this. In a word, oppression comes from without; demon possession comes from within. The devil can—from outside you—put oppressive suggestions into your mind. If you do not reject them immediately, they will find a place in your mind that militates against your joy and peace. People who suffer from depression may suffer from demonic oppression.

It is my pastoral judgment that people who are depressed are more likely *oppressed* by the devil, but not possessed. Overcoming this state comes by resisting the devil. Here are the three Rs regarding the devil: *recognize, refuse, resist.*

- Recognize the devil's suggestion: it will be something negative and fearful.
- Reject all negative thoughts and all fear; refuse to think about such.
- Don't give in to negative thoughts. Resist them.

Keep it up. The devil will see he is getting nowhere with you and will leave you. These things said, there is a place for responsible counseling if you can find a godly person who is competent to do this. I myself have had some counseling over the past number of years, and I thank God for it. See your pastor or church leader who can advise you.

Demon possession is a state whereby one is virtually controlled by an evil spirit or demon. People with a background of witchcraft or fortune-telling are most susceptible to this. Demon possession is very common in the third world, but with people consulting astrology charts and playing around with fortune-telling as they do nowadays, it is more common in America and in the UK than one might at first suppose. That said, demon possession is probably cured by only two things:

1. A responsible person who has the gift of the Holy Spirit to cast out demons
2. Total forgiveness

Caution: even if a demon has been cast out, one must *immediately* practice total forgiveness or the devil will return with seven more spirits that are more wicked, "and the last state of that person is worse than the first" (Matt. 12:45, ESV). At the end of the day total forgiveness is the way forward. The devil cannot dwell long in a person who has been completely eradicated of bitterness. Remember, total forgiveness is an act of the will. Mind you, total forgiveness is a major accomplishment; it is like climbing Mount Everest. Few do it. But you can do it by the mercy and help of the Holy Spirit.

2. Demon Possession Is a No-Joke Thing

This is a very serious matter. This happens when a person is virtually controlled by Satan. Two demon-possessed people who met Jesus were "so violent that no one could pass that way" (Matt. 8:28). The man described in the Gospel of Mark was so violent that no one could bind him, even with a chain. He had often been chained hand and foot, "but he tore the chains apart and broke the irons on his feet" (Mark 5:3–4). Living in tombs he would cry out and cut himself with stones (v. 5). When I say "virtually controlled by Satan," it is because a demon-possessed person at least has the presence of mind to want help! "When he saw Jesus from a distance, he ran and fell on his knees in front of him" (v. 6). Had he been totally controlled by Satan, he would not have been able to run to Jesus.

This shows that demon-possessed people want help. They may seem to be people who do not want help. They can be obnoxious. But they need help and want help if it is right there in front of them.

One of the first persons my wife led to Jesus through our Pilot Light ministry at Westminster Chapel was named Anthony, but he wanted to be called Tony. He came to me a week after he was converted. He said that there were razor blades cutting up his stomach. He was pale and in obvious pain. He then said to me with a shameful look on his face, "I have attended a black mass." In a split second I was given presence of mind.

While silently and fervently praying, "Jesus, cover me with Your precious blood," I said, "Tony, look at me." He looked at me as I began repeating over and over: "Jesus Christ is come in the flesh." A look of terror and horror appeared on his face as he exclaimed "Oh, oh, oh, oh!" I said, "In the name of Jesus Christ come out of him and go to your place of appointment and do not return."

Tony went limp. I took him inside Westminster Chapel and had him sit on a pew. In a few minutes he came out with color on his face and a big smile. "I don't know what you did, but I feel so good inside," he said.

That is my sole experience with casting out a demon. So far. And as I say in my book *Holy Fire* (in which I related the above story), it was Dr. Martyn Lloyd-Jones who told me what to do when you come face to face with a demon-possessed person. He said first, pray for your own protection, then start repeating aloud, "Jesus Christ is come in the flesh," and then prepare for a violent reaction. How right he was.

3. Casting Out Demons Is Not a Game

The sons of Sceva thought it was a fun thing to do to go around casting out devils. How they recognized the demon-possessed persons is not known. Perhaps they went looking for them. Perhaps they knew where they could be found. The previously mentioned case in the Gospels lived in tombs. Perhaps today they hang out in places where blatant wickedness prevails. With drug people. Prostitutes. Fortune-tellers. I suppose the sons of Sceva were looking for strange, weird, fearful, and dangerous-looking people. These would be people you would not want to be around or spend time with.

And yet people involved in witchcraft today might be pleasant and good-looking. Never forget that the devil "masquerades as an angel of light" (2 Cor. 11:14)—which could refer not only to false teachers but also to people who appear to be normal and sophisticated. They might be movie stars, bankers, politicians, entertainers, or rock stars. Some would call them beautiful people. The jet-setters. Yes. Do not think that demon-possessed people always look disheveled and unkempt.

At any rate, the sons of Sceva seemed to know how to find demon-possessed people, and they went up to them to see what might happen. They had a liturgy they thought would work, "In the name of the Jesus whom Paul preaches, I command you to come out" (Acts 19:13). It worked—at least up to a point. The demon was not exorcised; the man instead had an unexpected violent reaction—and unusual strength. Had the demon been exorcised, the man would not have overpowered those sons of Sceva. He would have been grateful and calm. Instead the demon-possessed man overpowered the sons of Sceva and left them naked and bleeding. There is no sign that a demon or demons ever left the poor man who got the liturgical treatment.

The sons of Sceva probably learned this liturgy from Paul—and then threw in Paul's name to the liturgy. Paul's way of doing this was to say, "In the name of Jesus Christ I command you to come out of her!" (Acts 16:18). So they added "whom Paul preaches" (Acts 19:13). What is more, what they did was almost certainly trying to make fun of Paul. These were Jews who hated Paul. But they apparently derived one thing from Paul—there was power in Jesus' name. Otherwise how would they know to cast out demons in Jesus' name? They were Jews. They were not Jews converted to Christ, or Luke would have said so. They were sons of a Jewish chief priest—at the top of the hierarchy in that area. And what a compliment to Paul! Wow. To be referred to as one who preaches the gospel and who casts out devils in Jesus' name. What a recommendation! They may also have seen Paul effectively cast out demons. In any case they seized the notion of Jesus' name and decided to see if it worked. But it backfired, as we will see further below.

By the way—slightly to change the subject: Do you know about those theologians and Bible teachers today who say of the Christian faith: Jesus, yes; Paul, no? This is the viewpoint of some liberal theologians who say we should follow the teachings of Jesus. Some say that Christianity would have done much better without Paul. Indeed, they say that Paul really "messed things up" and that it is a great pity that Saul of Tarsus was converted and then wrote all those letters. They assume that these letters (whether Galatians, Romans, Ephesians, 1 and 2 Corinthians) gave Christianity a bad direction. Shame on people who talk like this! But now think about this: the demons have let us know what the evil world thinks of Paul! They put Paul alongside Jesus: "Jesus I know, and Paul I know about" (Acts 19:15). That the *demons* would affirm Paul like this tells you all you need to know about Paul. They hated Jesus. They hated Paul. If the devil hates Paul, that is the highest recommendation Paul could get!

This is why I want to be famous in hell.

The ministry of casting out demons is dangerous business. Avoid it if you can. As Charles Spurgeon (1834–1892) said regarding the question whether one should go into the ministry of preaching the gospel, "If you can do anything else, do it." He said this because the call to preach the gospel is not for fence straddlers who aren't sure God called them. The full-time preaching ministry is not fun. It is not glamorous. It is full of hard work, rejection, unexpected pitfalls, huge responsibility—not to mention persecution. So, says Spurgeon, don't go there if there is something else you can do. This is surely true with the ministry of exorcism—casting out evil spirits. It is a no-joke thing. It is fraught with all kinds of testing. And potential danger. It is not for children. If you can do anything else, do it.

The need for patience and wisdom

The apostle Paul showed great wisdom when it came to this matter. Whereas there may be some who see a demon on every bush and rub their hands with glee at the prospect of confronting a demon-possessed person, Paul was the opposite. Luke wrote:

> Once when we were going to the place of prayer, we were met by a female slave who had a spirit by which she predicted the future. She earned a great deal of money for her owners by fortune-telling. She followed Paul and the rest of us, shouting, "These men are servants of the Most High God, who are telling you the way to be saved." She kept this up for many days. Finally Paul became so annoyed that he turned around and said to the spirit, "In the name of Jesus Christ I command you to come out of her!" At that moment the spirit left her.
>
> —Acts 16:16–18

Why did not Paul exorcise the demon the first day? Why did he wait? The slave girl kept shouting "for many days." Whyever did Paul not turn around immediately and cast out the demon? Part of the answer is a mystery, for it would seem reasonable had Paul cast the demon out at once. But perhaps he wanted to be absolutely sure that the slave girl was demonized and not mentally ill. Or perhaps she did not sufficiently interfere with his ministry at first. Or perhaps Paul wanted to be sure the demon was sufficiently agitated. It is possible that a demon-possessed person could have an evil spirit that lies dormant, as it were. This would be when the evil spirit in a person is not sufficiently stirred up. Such a person whose demon is not angry or annoyed might not be a candidate for an exorcism at a particular time.

The very presence of Jesus was sufficient to cause a demon to manifest (Mark 1:21–24). The presence of Paul caused the slave girl to begin manifesting. He was only going into a place or prayer (Acts 16:16).

Years ago, early in my ministry at Westminster Chapel, a man—clearly demon possessed—manifested during the evening service. It happened twice over several weeks. He interrupted the service each time, shouting loudly and using the vilest language you could imagine. Everybody heard him, possibly even people outside. As he kept shouting, some stewards gently led him out of the church building.

If that incident had taken place later in my ministry at Westminster Chapel I am quite sure I would have immediately walked back to the pew where he was shouting and tried to cast out the demon then and there.

After the incident happened the second time, I wanted to stop this from happening again. I sought to do something the following week. Some people knew who he was, and we tracked him down. We discovered he had been put in a hospital. Dr. Lloyd-Jones was alive at the time, and I asked for his advice. He suggested that I take a particular man he knew—an Elim Pentecostal (a UK-based Pentecostal denomination) pastor and go to the hospital to exorcise the demon. But when this pastor and I were allowed to see the man in hospital, it turned out the man was heavily drugged. He was extremely calm and polite. He vaguely knew who I was. And nothing worked. Our chanting, "Jesus Christ is come in the flesh," several times came to nothing. He actually fell asleep. We left feeling a bit stupid and certainly defeated!

We learned from this experience that if the demon in a person is apparently calm, one may be less likely to succeed in the exorcism. One must probably wait until the evil spirit manifests.

This may be why Paul waited. If the demon was therefore not sufficiently agitated, Paul would almost certainly have ignored her. But he waited. He showed great patience. He eventually became "greatly annoyed" (Acts 16:18, ESV). And then he cast the demon out. It is a lesson for people who are in this kind of ministry to learn. In the previously mentioned case when I had my only experience in casting out a demon, you will recall that my repeated chant, "Jesus Christ is come in the flesh," stirred up the man and the demon came out immediately.

4. Demons Dwell in the World of Tartarus

The angels are in chains awaiting the day of judgment. But despite their being in chains, they were free to roam with limitations in order to do damage to the gospel of Jesus Christ. This shows that God permitted them to exist in this way. They were in chains; they could go only so far. But far enough to try to thwart God's purpose. Why would God allow this? I can only answer: His ways are higher than our ways, His thoughts higher than our thoughts (Isa. 55:9). We cannot figure everything out. This means also that the world of Tartarus—an invisible world—is all around us. For that reason you and I should pray continually for protection against the devil and his fallen angels. Do you pray for protection? You should.

The first thing I do every morning—no exception—is to pray for the blood of Jesus to be sprinkled on Louise and me and all members of my family. I call each of them by name. I pray it again each evening before I go to sleep.

When my friend in England Evangelist J. John goes into a hotel room, he "cleanses" it—asking God to sprinkle the room with the blood of Jesus by the Holy Spirit. Following Charles Carrin's example, when I step on an airplane, I lay my hand on the plane! When Louise and I first moved into our home in Hendersonville, Tennessee, we prayed for the sprinkling of the blood of Jesus on the entire house and property and every room. When I take a trip, I pray for the sprinkling of the blood of Christ on the car and the traffic. I pray the same when I see my doctor for his wisdom or for the surgeon if I need an operation. I pray this for my grandsons when they watch videos. It is something we have done for years. Highly recommended to you!

The devil and his angels are in Tartarus as punishment for their revolt against God. They left their home in glory for a home in "gloomy dungeons" (2 Pet. 2:4, ESV). They are in "darkness" (Jude 6). After the day of judgment they will be sent to "eternal fire prepared for the devil and his angels" (Matt. 25:41). They know that the time is short, and in the meantime they are "filled with fury" (Rev. 12:12). They are angry, fearful, and vengeful, hoping to take billions to everlasting hell with them. Their goal is to enter high places and influence heads of nations, those who control government, entertainment, the world of sports, education, money, and politics. They want to stop the gospel from being proclaimed. They want to popularize everything from abortions to pornography. Whenever they can, they enter human beings created in the image of God because of their hatred for God and His Son. That is the background for demon possession. And, what is more, they want to keep Christians from joy—by oppression.

Can a Christian have a demon? In my book *Holy Fire* I tell the story of Dr. Martyn Lloyd-Jones, who advised some Welsh elders to cast a demon out of a Christian woman he knew. Hudson Taylor (1832–1905), the great missionary to China, cast a demon out of a person. The next day Taylor was partially paralyzed. He realized that he did not remember to pray for protection and, strange as it may seem, a demon had entered him. He got Christians around him to cast the demon out of him. They did. It left.

The world of Tartarus is a strange, invisible, and largely unknowable world. I say it again: don't try to figure it out. God has told us all we need to know.

5. Casting Out Demons Is an Enterprise of the Godly Not the Worldly

The folly of the seven sons of Sceva is a lesson to all. When it comes to the ministry of casting out devils, "no trespassing" is the rule of thumb. This ministry is only for the Christian—but the fully committed Christian. It is not for the novice. It is not for the uneducated. It is not for the immature. The ministry of casting out demons is not only for the Spirit-filled but also for one with wisdom. You can be Spirit-filled and lack wisdom. This is why the initial qualifications for the first deacons were for men who are "full of the Spirit *and* wisdom" (Acts 6:3, emphasis added).

The seven sons of Sceva were not even Christians, not to mention being Spirit-filled or men of wisdom. They were foolish men. Stupid. So will you be if you enter such an arena as this if you are not called of God to do so. The Peter principle applies here: in a hierarchy people tend to be promoted to the level of their incompetence. This is because some are pushed to take a position for which they are not qualified, or they push themselves to take a position which they are not able to do. So if you, my friend, try to cast out a demon and are not called of God to do so, you are promoting yourself to the level of your incompetence and will be very sorry.

I know a fairly well-known preacher who had a ministry of "stomping on the devil" when he would conduct meetings. He would get everybody to do it on signal, leading the whole congregation to do it together. He decided one day to take on San Francisco with all its sin and debauchery. Bad move. He suffered greatly for it, although I am not sure he sees this as the reason.

Spiritual warfare is meant to be essentially defensive. This means we don't go around looking for a fight. We do not take the offense. The devil does this with us. That's his job description. He is the "accuser" of all believers (Rev. 12:10). Accusing is what he does. Rule of thumb, believe me, don't ever pick a fight with the devil. You have no promise of victory if you pick a fight with him; you will be in over your head, out of your depth. You are no match for Satan. But if he picks a fight with you, you have the promise of God. You have God on your side. Here below is the classic passage in the Bible regarding spiritual warfare. You will see that spiritual warfare is defensive; it is carried out when you have been attacked by the devil. That is when you apply these verses—and take your "stand."

> Put on the full armor of God, so that you can take your *stand* against the devil's schemes. For our struggle is not against flesh and blood, but against the rulers, against the authorities, against the powers of this dark world and against the spiritual forces of evil in the heavenly realms. Therefore put on the full armor of God, so that when the day of evil comes, you may be able to *stand* your ground, and after you have done everything, to *stand*. *Stand* firm then, with the belt of truth buckled around your waist, with the breastplate of righteousness in place, and with your feet fitted with the readiness that comes from the gospel of peace.
>
> —Ephesians 6:11–15, emphasis added

The word *stand* appears four times in this fundamental lesson on spiritual warfare. What do you do when Satan attacks? Stand. What do you do when the evil day comes? Stand. What do you do when all hell breaks loose and the heat is almost overwhelming? Stand. What do you do when you are lied about, knowing it is an attack of the devil? Stand. When you are under attack, you are not required to make progress; you stand. You don't walk. You don't go backward. You don't fall. You stand. So if you manage merely to *stand* when the evil day comes, *that is great progress*. Remember this the next time you are under a satanic attack: just stand. Do that, and you win.

6. There Is Power in the Name of Jesus

Think about this: the unbelieving Jews who wanted to use the name of Jesus—having no devotion to Christ whatever—brought on a demonstration of the demonic they were not prepared for. They said, "In the name of the Jesus whom Paul preaches, I command you to come out" (Acts 19:13). They had the liturgy down to the letter. They learned it well. Their problem was to underestimate the sheer *power of that name*. Two things followed. First, the evil spirit answered them. I don't think they were expecting that. He answered them in their own language—presumably Greek: "Jesus I know, and Paul I know about, but who are you?" (Acts 19:15). The power of Jesus' name was unwittingly demonstrated; the evil spirit inside the man spoke out. He recognized the names of both men—Jesus and Paul. But he did not recognize the strange person who invoked the name of Jesus. But it evoked a surprising response—intelligible words that they understood. The demons had no idea who these men were who used the name of Jesus.

Second, their invoking the name of Jesus got another astonishing response: the demon-possessed man jumped on them and overpowered them all. The seven sons of Sceva got one thing right: they found a man who was truly demon possessed. But the evil spirit inside him took over and gave him strength that was unnatural, leaving these seven Jews humiliated. The demon-possessed man tore off their clothes, leaving them naked and bleeding. That came merely from the use of the name, even if they were trying to have fun.

Think about this too: if unbelieving Jews can invoke the name of Jesus and cause such a stir as we have just observed, how much more power should we believers have in invoking the name of Jesus!

But consider what power will be in that name when on the

last day the name of Jesus is invoked before the angels, the fallen angels, the saved, and the lost.

> That at the name of Jesus every knee should bow,
> in heaven and on earth and under the earth,
> and every tongue acknowledge that Jesus Christ is Lord,
> to the glory of God the Father.
>
> —Philippians 2:10–11

In the meantime we can all sing:

> All hail the pow'r of Jesus' name!
> Let angels prostrate fall;
> Bring forth the royal diadem,
> And crown Him Lord of all!
>
> Oh, that with yonder sacred throng
> We at His feet may fall!
> We'll join the everlasting song,
> And crown Him Lord of all!
>
> —Edward Perronet (1726–1792)

7. Tartarus Is a World of Its Own

Tartarus is a world of its own in which its inhabitants—from Satan to the least significant demon—know what is going on in our world. However, the devil is not omniscient. Only God knows everything. The devil's knowledge is limited. He is limited to what is in the past and present. He knows a lot. But only God knows *everything*—the future as perfectly as the past. The true prophets of God foretold certain things in the future because God knows the future perfectly.

The devil does not know the future; he can only predict based upon knowledge of people's minds in the *present*. However, some will point out that the slave girl had a spirit "by which she predicted the future" (Acts 16:16). But that is all she could do—predict. Prediction is one thing; infallible foretelling all that will literally happen is another. When she was delivered of the demon, "her owners realized that their hope of making money was gone" (Acts 16:19). On the surface some would argue that this proves that the devil knows the future. No. It shows she lost the ability to know what is in people's minds. Until she was delivered, she could read people's minds. It is a satanic gift that some demon-possessed people have. Some of them boast that they know the future, but they only know what is in some people's minds in the present. If one knows what is in people's minds, he or she has a high level knowledge of probability of what they will do.

Therefore a closer examination would reveal that:

1. The devil only knows what *is* going on in people's minds
2. Through this knowledge of the present the devil can *predict* what will *possibly* happen

But the slave girl no doubt got it right a lot. This is what fortune-tellers do. It is what astrology charts purport to do. It is what a clairvoyant does now and then. A gift through the demonic knowledge of what is in people's minds no doubt gets it right a good deal of the time. Such a prediction, however, is based upon probability. In other words, the evil spirit *predicts* but does not infallibly foretell. People like this tell you when they get it right; they don't tell you when they miss it. If the devil knew the future perfectly, demon-possessed people could always win in gambling—from casinos to horse racing. What Satan knows is not the way the dice will roll or what horse will win but what is in *people's* minds—both friends and enemies—in the *present*. With this kind of knowledge one can often predict accurately what will happen.

The seven sons of Sceva knew nothing about the demonic world, which the New Testament identifies as Tartarus. These Jewish would-be exorcists had no knowledge of the existence of demons that are not only conscious but knowledgeable of things going on in our world. But for some reason their invoking Jesus' name raised the curiosity of these evil spirits. Such spirits, or demons, like Satan himself—the top honcho in Tartarus—are very intelligent beings. They were very familiar with Jesus. They knew who He was as soon as He began ministering about the kingdom of heaven. Jesus spoke with great authority, not as the teachers of the law. As we just saw above, Jesus was *teaching*, not even casting out evil spirits, and still He caused a man with an evil spirit to cry out, "What do you want with us, Jesus of Nazareth? Have you come to destroy us? I know who you are—the Holy One of God!" (Mark 1:24). In other words, the very presence of Jesus precipitated a terrified response from an evil spirit without Him doing anything but teaching! This shows that the world of Tartarus—inhabited by the hierarchy of evil spirits from Satan down to the most insignificant demon—was fully conscious of Jesus' presence on the earth. All it took for this to be known was for a demon-possessed man to be in Jesus' presence. The demon manifested before Jesus took the opportunity to cast him out. Then Jesus ordered the evil spirit, "'Be quiet!...Come out of him!' The impure spirit shook the man violently and came out of him with a shriek" (vv. 25–26).

This shows that the very presence of the Holy Spirit can stir up demons without there being an overt ministry of exorcisms. The power of the Spirit stirs up demons. The power of the Spirit makes them nervous. They live in nonstop terror when the presence of Jesus—the presence of the Holy Spirit—is manifesting with authority and power. Therefore, when the demon spoke out, "Jesus I know," it was mirroring the knowledge of the entire population of evil spirits—billions and billions—in Tartarus. The whole world of Tartarus knew who Jesus was. Jesus was the most feared person of all. From Satan to the least powerful demon in the spirit world the knowledge of Jesus of Nazareth was the governing force that kept them in perpetual fear.

But what about Paul? The evil spirit added, "I know about Paul" (Greek *epistamai*—"I am acquainted with Paul"). This is because Paul had gained a reputation in hell—Tartarus. What Paul had been doing through fearless and uncompromising preaching, teaching, leading people to a saving knowledge of Jesus Christ, plus casting out demons, made him known throughout this dark, gloomy world of Tartarus. It is one of the highest compliments that can be paid to a Christian—to be famous in hell. I so wish it were true of me. It is probable that Paul—next to Jesus—was the most famous person in hell—Tartarus.

It was one thing for Jesus to have appeared on earth—teaching, preaching, healing, agitating the powers that be in Jerusalem, plus casting out devils. These things terrified Satan and his angels. But there was more. Jesus died on the cross, which the demonic world rejoiced over initially, thinking it was their accomplishment. But when Saul of Tarsus was converted, oh dear. What a blow to the satanic kingdom. Saul of Tarsus had possibly been the chief agent on earth who represented the purpose of Satan and his angels. But he was converted to Satan's archenemy, the Lord Jesus Christ. This sent tremors throughout the world of Tartarus. The conversion of Saul alone would have terrified the devil and all evil spirits. What is more, Paul immediately began preaching the good news of Jesus and before long was engaged in the ministry of deliverance. No wonder, then, that the evil spirit would cry out, "I am acquainted with Paul!"

But the evil spirit was not remotely aware of the seven sons of Sceva. These Jews were Johnny-come-latelys. Newcomers. Upstarts. Novices. Out of their depth. "Who are you?" they asked. The world of Tartarus did not recognize these men coming from out of the blue, trying to penetrate the satanic world. They had no authority to do what they were trying to do. *Only Christians* who have been given this mandate dare enter this arena. The evil spirit therefore did not recognize these seven Jews who invoked the name of Jesus whom Paul preached. Not only that; the demon in this poor man was not about to obey this injunction that it come out. The demon was not only not intimidated by these seven Jews, he attacked them!

The devil has billions of his agents scattered all over the earth. I don't know how the hierarchy of the satanic world works. Nobody knows. C. S. Lewis' *Screwtape Letters* is recommended, but is not to be taken too seriously as the final manual of how to know Satan's devices. I wish for example he had put in his extraordinary book that Satan does not want you to read the Bible—huge omission. And yet you can be sure that Satan is at the top, calling the shots with the billions of demons under him. Through them Satan seeks to mastermind the world. Even the weather if he can; he is called the "prince and power of the air" (Eph. 2:2, ESV). God is ultimately in charge, however, and Satan is his tool. Satan can do *nothing*—ever—without God's permission (Job 1). All Satan does will eventually bring honor and glory to God. Satan always overreaches himself when he is recognized, refused, and resisted. Always.

Satan seeks control of governments, the media, the banking systems, education—universities and seminaries—and wants to turn Bible-believing Evangelicals into liberals who deny the blood of Jesus, not to mention the existence of heaven and hell. The devil knows what is going on in the world, what is in the minds of heads of state and what their aims are. He knows what is in the minds of those who control the media, TV, and newspapers. He is totally behind those who put pornography on the internet. He knows what is in the hearts and motives of those who control the banking systems. He seeks to divide families. He will chase after the new convert to Christ with a vengeance. But never forget:

greater is Jesus who is in us by the Holy Spirit than he who is in the world!

The evil spirit of Tartarus knew Jesus, that is, all the inhabitants of the satanic world were very aware of Jesus. He was famous throughout the world of Tartarus. And the evil spirit quickly recognized the name of Paul when his name was brought into the liturgy. But the evil spirit was *unafraid* of the men who tried to exorcise it.

The question is: Does the world of Tartarus know about you and me? Jesus was famous in hell. Paul was famous in hell. But are you and I known in hell?

I want to be famous in hell. I fear that the evil forces of the demonic world are not aware of me at all.

Chapter 10

CELEBRATING IN HELL

Tell it not in Gath, proclaim it not in the streets of Ashkelon, lest the daughters of the Philistines be glad, lest the daughters of the uncircumcised rejoice.

—2 Samuel 1:20

The last thing a follower of Jesus would want is to give the devil any pleasure. Not that there is any pleasure in the world of Tartarus. We have seen that Tartarus is a place of doom and gloom, and there is no true joy there. So I ask the reader to bear with me; this is a tongue-in-cheek use of the word *celebrating* in the present chapter. We do know that there are times of celebrating in the "presence of the angels over one sinner who repents" (Luke 15:10). Therefore, it just might be possible there is an equivalent of celebrating in hell.

At any rate, any celebration in hell is temporary.

But if we give in to unbelief, it pleases Satan. If we question God's Word—its infallibility and integrity—it pleases the devil. When a Christian falls into sin, it gives the devil pleasure. When a church leader loses credibility by sexual misconduct or dishonesty with finances, the devil is delighted. When the world does not respect the church but thumbs its nose at us, there is pleasure in the demonic world. When there is no fear of God in the church, Satan is at ease.

One of the best ways to know the will of God is to imagine what would please the devil, then do the opposite—and you will be safe. Satan exists to get true believers to disobey God, to get vengeance toward God. He was cast down from his former estate (2 Pet. 2:4; Rev. 12:10). He knows his doom is sealed. But he wants to do all the damage he possibly can do to God and His people in the meantime. This is what he lives for, if I may put it like that. He hates God with a depth and determination that cannot be adequately put in words. He hates the triune God, he hates the people of God, he hates those who want to honor God, and he hates it when people praise Jesus Christ—his archenemy. Likewise then, he loves it when people do not praise God or when God's people lose heart, when church attendance is low, and when people are not being saved.

Those who contribute to the lack of power and authority in the church of God are therefore popular in Tartarus and give the satanic world cause for celebration. Those who lead the way in getting people to doubt God's Word are popular in hell. When a nation loses its way—having been largely influenced by biblical standards—Satan rejoices. Those who support abortion, pornography, drug addiction, prostitution, the disintegration of the family, and lead the way in bringing a nation down, down, down are popular in hell.

Satan is looking high and low throughout the world for those who will be his agents in society. He wants to destroy decency, honor, uprightness, morality, integrity, and clean living all over the world. Those who assist him in this endeavor are popular in hell. This gives the world of Tartarus cause for celebration.

"Righteousness exalts a nation, but sin condemns any people"

(Prov. 14:34). "Blessed is the nation whose God is the Lord, the people he chose for his inheritance" (Ps. 33:12). But when a nation turns its back on God, and sin elbows its way into society and the church, you can be sure that hell rejoices.

The last thing we should want is to give the devil pleasure. David put it this way: "Do not let me be put to shame, nor let my enemies triumph over me" (Ps. 25:2).

"Tell It Not in Gath"—a Proverb in Israel

When ancient Israel lost to the Philistines in King Saul's day, it was a sad moment for the Israelites and for David. Although Saul had sought to destroy David, David mourned at the death of Saul (2 Sam. 1). King Saul, who had been "yesterday's man" for some twenty years, was a complete failure. Things went from bad to worse. After outlawing witches and fortune-tellers, Saul turned to the witch of Endor for sustenance (1 Sam. 28). When the Philistines were closing in on him, he committed suicide (1 Sam. 31). It was a sad day in Israel. When David got the news of Saul's tragic end, he said, "Tell it not in Gath" (2 Sam. 1:20). Those words became a proverb in Israel (Mic. 1:10).

Gath was one of the five major cities in the Philistine territory. But Gath was not as strong as it once was. David did not want to give any of the Philistines cause for rejoicing, certainly not Gath, a city that would have wanted to come back strong again. So when David said, "Tell it not in Gath," he did not want the horrible news of Israel's shame and defeat to reach that city lest they have cause to rejoice.

This phrase became a proverb in Israel. It meant *keep the enemy from hearing our bad news lest they rejoice.*

We should feel the same way, that is, we do not want to give our enemy—the devil—cause to rejoice. Bad news for the people of God is good news for Satan. Weakness in the church of God is good news for the devil. Those who would keep the church impotent, losing credibility, having a form of godliness while denying its power (2 Tim. 3:5) are, in a word, popular in hell.

Royalty in the Bible

Pharaoh of Egypt

> Then a new king, to whom Joseph meant nothing, came to power in Egypt.
>
> —Exodus 1:8

This verse is one of the most ominous, even prophetic and sadly repeated descriptions of almost every generation of the church or regarding a new work of God, as in a new denomination. It is so often true that the first generation of a movement has the power and favor of God, the second generation has about half that, the third a pale imitation. By then the state of the church or what at one time had been a very hopeful work of God is often unrecognizable.

The original account of King Pharaoh and Joseph refers to the extraordinary favor given by the king to Joseph and his family. Never had a pharaoh been so appreciative of someone as the pharaoh who gave Joseph power and favor, second only to the king himself (Gen. 41:44). The entire family of Joseph was warmly welcomed in Egypt and given the land of Goshen for a home. But after several generations the Israelites multiplied and became a threat to the existing king, hence that scary description, "there arose a king...who did not know Joseph" (esv). He was not indebted to Joseph. The Israelites were no longer needed nor appreciated. Pharaoh was possibly unaware but certainly now ungrateful for the contribution Joseph and the Israelites made to Egypt years before. As we would say today, the new pharaoh threw the Israelites under the bus.

Because Israel was under the special covenant of the Most High, the king, Pharaoh, became popular in hell. However, being popular in hell is not necessarily a permanent condition. Situations change. Nations change. God is over all.

> No one from the east or the west
> or from the desert can exalt themselves.
> It is God who judges:
> He brings one down, he exalts another.
> —Psalm 75:6–7

> Surely the nations are like a drop in a bucket;
> they are regarded as dust on the scales;
> he weighs the islands as though they were fine dust.
> —Isaiah 40:15

King Rehoboam

The successor to his father, Solomon, Rehoboam had a hard act to follow. Indeed, "The Lord highly exalted Solomon in the sight of all Israel and bestowed on him royal splendor such as no king over Israel ever had before" (1 Chron. 29:25). Rather than rejoice in his father's blessing and greatness, Rehoboam was threatened by it. As Pharaoh was threatened by the growing number of the Israelites, Rehoboam was threatened by the acclaim and glory his father was given. He was foolishly determined to outdo his father and prove that he was greater than Solomon. "My little finger is thicker than my father's waist," Rehoboam declared (2 Chron. 10:10).

Rehoboam was popular in hell. His foolish pride and jealousy led to Judah's and Israel's eventual split down the road. The nation that God had raised up was eventually divided—never to be the same again. It began with an insecure, incompetent, and jealous king. Rehoboam was totally unteachable and unreachable. "Who can stand before jealousy?" (Prov. 27:4). It was jealousy that motivated Lucifer to revolt against God; it was jealousy that lay behind the crucifixion of Jesus (Mark 15:10). It was jealousy that infuriated the Jews as the number of Christians grew (Acts 13:45).

Jealousy is popular in hell. It is partly what holds the demonic world together. When you are the object of jealousy, there is nothing you can do to change those who are jealous of you. You can flatter them, brag on them, get people to talk to them, or shame them! It won't work. Jealousy is the essence of most satanic attacks. When the attack comes, what do you do? Just stand. This is the way we are told to engage in spiritual warfare. (See Ephesians 6:10–14.) You stand. Don't fight. Don't trip or fall. Just stand. Remember, the greatest freedom is having nothing to prove.

Rehoboam was going to prove that he was greater than his father. So silly. But this is repeated thousands of times—in politics, in education, in medicine, in law, in the church. A pastor often needs to prove he is greater than his predecessor and sometimes says things about that person that are not very nice. A politician wants to show he is abler than the person he followed and often blames his predecessor for his own lack of progress.

Caution: do your best to come to terms with your own jealousy. It is easy to see in others, very difficult to admit it is your problem. (See my book *Jealousy—The Sin No One Talks About*.) In any case remember, jealousy is born in hell and gets its impetus there.

After Judah and Israel were divided, Judah had a succession of twenty kings—eight good ones, twelve bad ones. Israel had nineteen kings, all bad.

Ahab and Jezebel, king and queen of Israel

It is difficult to say who was more evil, King Ahab or his domineering wife, Queen Jezebel. It is said of Ahab that he "did more evil in the eyes of the LORD than any of those before him" (1 Kings 16:30). Ahab was the son of Omri, who "did evil in the eyes of the LORD and sinned more than all those before him" (v. 25). All the evil kings of Israel gave cause for celebration in hell, but Queen Jezebel would almost certainly win the prize for being the most wicked of any royal figure—from Judah or Israel. The world of Tartarus must have rejoiced over the evil that this couple perpetrated.

Ahab and Jezebel are proof that miracles will not necessarily convince people to turn to God. Elijah the prophet, the most extraordinary prophet of Israel next to Moses, openly called fire down from heaven before all the people. It caused the people generally to fall prostrate and cry out, "The LORD—he is God! The LORD—he is God!" (1 Kings 18:38–39). This was one of the high-water marks of ancient Israelite history. Human reason might conclude that an undoubted miracle like that will prove that there is a God and that all people—kings, queens, rich, famous—would immediately turn to Him if a miracle happened before their eyes. No. Ahab merely told Jezebel how Elijah destroyed the false prophets. Instead of their turning to God, Jezebel sent a messenger to Elijah saying, "May the gods deal with me, be it ever so severely, if by this time tomorrow I do not make your life like one of them"—that is, like the prophets of Baal who were slain (1 Kings 19:1–2). She failed to get rid of Elijah, who had been protected by God. But this account shows how an unquestioned miracle will not change a heart unless God sovereignly changes a person.

Sometime later Ahab was found sulking because Naboth would not sell his property to the king. Jezebel scolded him: "Is this how you act as king over Israel? Get up and eat! Cheer up! I'll get you the vineyard of Naboth" (1 Kings 21:5–7). She then coerced two men to declare falsely that Naboth had blasphemed against God. The innocent Naboth was consequently stoned to death. Then Jezebel said to her husband, "Get up and take possession of the vineyard of Naboth" (v. 15).

Ahab and Jezebel demonstrated how low wicked and unjust evil may stoop to. It shows what the human heart is capable of doing. It shows how a wicked person can have a seared conscience and feel no guilt whatever from such a heinous thing.

But such wickedness is popular in hell. There is no depth of sin, no extent of evil, no limit of what is painful and horrible that the world of Tartarus does not gloat about. Human words fail—even to come close—to describe the extreme possibility of evil and suffering caused by Satan.

The more wicked the event on earth, the more cause for celebration in hell. The more evil the person, the more popular they are in hell. Satan loves it.

King Herod I

Known as Herod the Great, this was the king who reigned at the time of Jesus' birth. Though known as king of Judea, he was loyal to Rome. When the magi from the East came following the star that they believed would lead them to the king of the Jews, they attracted a lot of attention. They asked, "Where is the one who has been born king of the Jews?" (Matt. 2:2). This got Herod's attention. Herod called the biblical scholars to ask where the Christ would be born. "In Bethlehem," came the answer (v. 5). Herod subsequently ordered that all male babies born in or near Bethlehem under the age of two be killed (v. 16).

You may be sure that Herod was popular in hell. Herod's vile act was possibly referred to by John when in his vision he saw that a "dragon stood in front of the woman who was about to give birth, so that it might devour her child the moment he was born"—a male child (Rev. 12:1–5). As we saw previously, Satan tried numerous times to kill Jesus. Those who made attempts to kill Him were popular in hell.

The Crucifixion of Jesus

Judas Iscariot

One of the twelve disciples, Judas was known by Jesus from the beginning as His betrayer (John 2:25; 13:11). Why Jesus chose Judas is a mystery no one can solve until we get to heaven. What is undoubted is that Satan "prompted" Judas to betray Jesus (John 13:2), and that soon afterward Satan "entered into him" (v. 27), meaning that Judas became demon-possessed. That would be enough to bring about celebration in hell.

At that moment I would guess that Judas Iscariot was the most celebrated human being in hell. Judas was orchestrated by Satan to carry out his evil deed. As we have seen previously, the devil masterminded the crucifixion of Christ, no doubt influencing not only Judas but the Jews, the chief priest, Herod Antipas, and Pontius Pilate. They all had a hand in it, Satan assuming he was the chief architect of the entire matter. But as we have seen already, the princes of this world had no idea what was going on or "they would not have crucified the Lord of glory" (1 Cor. 2:8).

The devil always overreaches himself, although the realization of this often takes time. It turns out that God was at the bottom of it all! Where sin abounds, grace does all the more abound. God knows the end from the beginning (Isa. 46:10). Satan does *nothing* without God allowing it; that is, the devil's evil deeds fall within the mystery of God's permission.

The most popular person in hell will sooner or later be exposed. For example, Elijah forecast the end of Ahab's descendants (1 Kings 21:21–22) and the violent death of Jezebel. Concerning Jezebel, "Dogs will devour Jezebel by the walls of Jezreel" (v. 23). That is exactly what happened (2 Kings 9:36–37).

Those who are popular in hell may well end up keeping company with Satan forever and ever. If such people are not granted repentance, they will be punished and spend their time in everlasting fire that was prepared for the devil and his angels (Matt. 25:41).

To choose to be popular on the earth risks being popular in hell—the worst place imaginable to be popular.

SATAN'S INTERFERENCE IN THE EARLY CHURCH

Ananias and Sapphira

There were two notable converts in the early church who wanted to be in with the high-profile Christians. This came when there was such power present that many Christians became utterly detached from material things. Some of them sold their possessions and gave all the money to the apostles for distribution to the needy. Ananias and Sapphira decided to get in with these more prominent disciples such as Barnabas (Acts 4:34–37). But their plan backfired—seriously backfired. They sold a piece of property, but "kept back part of the money" for themselves (Acts 5:1–2). I reckon that in a non-revival situation this couple would have gotten away with their plan. But they made their mistake by their deceit with so much power present. Simon Peter immediately picked up on this, saying to Ananias, "How is it that *Satan has so filled your heart* that you have lied to the Holy Spirit and have kept for yourself some of the money you received for the land?" Peter added, "You have not lied just to human beings but to God" (vv. 3–4, emphasis added). Immediately Ananias was struck dead on the spot. The same thing was true regarding his wife, Sapphira. Three hours later she came in, not knowing what had happened. After lying about the money she too was struck dead (vv. 7–10).

Ananias and Sapphira wanted to be popular on earth—in this case with the leaders in the early church.

There have always been people like this. They want to be in with the more prominent believers—whether church leaders, the clergy, or prominent laypeople. It seems a harmless thing. It happens all the time. But today, I suspect, we are not in a revival situation, and those elbowing in for prominence get away with it.

But in a revival situation, which was very present in the case in Acts 5, Satan looks for ways to disrupt the unity. He appeals to our pride and the need to be seen with the most important people. Those who want to be popular on the earth—even in the church—by deceitful behavior, risk giving Satan cause to celebrate and therefore become popular in hell. This is why Peter said that Satan filled the hearts of Ananias and Sapphira.

However, as we have seen, Satan always overreaches himself. One might have thought that such "fear" that came on all the church (v. 11) would scare people off! I sometimes think that many in the church today want to keep things neat and tidy so that people will not be afraid to come to church. The truth is, never has the church, speaking generally, been so neat and tidy as it is at the present time, yet church attendance has been on the wane for years in many places. As to what happened after the Ananias and Sapphira scenario, "more and more men and women believed in the Lord and were added to their number" (v. 14)!

The origin of deacons

The first quarrel in the church (that we know of) happened when jealousy crept in. As we saw earlier, jealousy is born in hell. It is what made Satan want to revolt against the Most High. Furthermore, Jonathan Edwards said that when the church is revived, so is the devil.

> In those days when the number of disciples was increasing, the Hellenistic Jews among them complained against the Hebraic Jews because their widows were being overlooked in the daily distribution of food.
>
> —Acts 6:1

There had always been a rivalry between Greek Jews and Hebraic Jews. The Hebrews possibly thought they were a cut above Greek Jews. Therefore when the Greek Jews felt left out, this rivalry surfaced. A major crisis loomed.

But the devil always overreaches himself. This incident led to the formation of deacons. The Twelve unanimously came up with a solution.

> It would not be right for us to neglect the ministry of the word of God in order to wait on tables. Brothers and sisters, choose seven men from among you who are known to be full of the Spirit and wisdom. We will turn this responsibility over to them and will give our attention to prayer and the ministry of the word.
>
> —ACTS 6:2–4

The result of this decision led to the church growing more than ever. "So the word of God spread. The number of disciples in Jerusalem increased rapidly, and a large number of priests became obedient to the faith" (v. 7). But there is more: Stephen, one of the seven, stood out. His knowledge of the Word enabled him to give a powerful address to the Sanhedrin (Acts 7). It led to Stephen being the first martyr of the church, but more than that, it ultimately played a role in the conversion of Saul of Tarsus. Saul witnessed Stephen being stoned and heard Stephen's last words, "Lord, do not hold this sin against them [i.e., those who stoned him]" (Acts 7:59–60). Saul of Tarsus was there, approving—if not directing—the entire episode. Later on, after his conversion, Saul admits to the effect Stephen's testimony had on him (Acts 22:20).

This is one more example of Satan overreaching himself. You can read on in the Book of Acts and see how God overruled again and again when trouble came to the church—whether with family quarrels, persecution, or satanic opposition. You will recall the case of the slave girl who kept annoying Paul, and who was exorcised of a demon (Acts 16:18). This brought severe opposition and persecution to Paul. But it also led to the sudden conversion of the Philippian jailer (vv. 22–34).

This goes to show that any celebration in hell—the world of Tartarus—is temporary. All satanic victories are temporary and will eventually expose Satan's folly.

> God made you alive with Christ. He forgave us all our sins, having canceled the charge of our legal indebtedness, which stood against us and condemned us; he has taken it away, nailing it to the cross. And having disarmed the powers and authorities, he made a public spectacle of them, triumphing over them by the cross.
>
> —Colossians 2:13–15

Satan with all his power is a defeated foe.

Chapter 11

THE DEVIL'S WORST NIGHTMARE

And when they could not find them, they dragged Jason and some of the brothers before the city authorities, shouting, "These men who have turned the world upside down have come here also."

—Acts 17:6, esv

A Christian woman I know decided to run for political office. She was elected to the House of Representatives in her state. The party that chose her to represent them apparently did not know all that she stood for. It turned out that among other things she stood vehemently against abortion. She caused no small stir in the House of Representatives generally and her political party particularly. The Speaker of the House called her into his office. He said to her: "You are the devil's worst nightmare." Wow.

I cannot imagine a greater compliment.

Her example reminds me of the great Chicago evangelist Dwight L. Moody (1837–1899). There is little doubt of his fame in hell or of the major nightmare his life caused the devil. It has been said that when he died in Northfield, Massachusetts, the word was echoed in Chicago newspapers that "the man who rid hell of millions died today."

We now take a further look at the crucifixion of Jesus. As we have already seen, Satan saw himself as the architect of the whole thing. It began with Jesus' being betrayed by Judas Iscariot. This led to Jesus' arrest. Jesus then made an interesting comment to the chief priest, the officers of the temple guard, and the elders who had come for him:

> Am I leading a rebellion, that you have come with swords and clubs? Every day I was with you in the temple courts, and you did not lay a hand on me. But this is your hour—when darkness reigns.
>
> —LUKE 22:52–53

Think of that. This is Jesus' own interpretation of His arrest and subsequent treatment: "This is your hour—when darkness reigns." He refers to the sinister plans of the chief priest and those wanting His death as being *their moment* but a moment orchestrated by "darkness"—meaning Satan.

To put it another way: the greatest and most wonderful thing to take place in the history of the world is Jesus' death on the cross; it is what saves us! And yet Jesus says that it took place "when darkness reigns." Figure that out.

This brings us to the word *antinomy*—two irreconcilable principles that are both true. J. I. Packer says that theologically the definition should be two principles that are "apparently" irreconcilable.[1] A good example of an antinomy is this: Jesus is God and man. He is not 50 percent God and 50 percent man, but 100 percent God and 100 percent man. Or take the truth of the sovereignty of God and evangelism. The sovereignty of God is His prerogative to do what He chooses to do with whomever He pleases, including whom He saves, yet evangelism is our mandate to preach the gospel to everyone. It is an antinomy.

This is what you have when you consider the crucifixion to be the invention of "darkness"—Jesus' word—and "Christ crucified" being the "power of God and the wisdom of God"—Paul's words (1 Cor. 1:24).

Who Crucified Jesus?

In recent years there has been considerable discussion regarding the question, "Who crucified Jesus?" For years the assumption has been that it was the Jews who crucified Him. No one questioned that for hundreds of years. But some Jews have protested this notion, hence the question has been re-asked. Some Jews resented being accused of orchestrating it. And yet there are at least five possibilities—all being true:

1. The Jews did it, led by the chief priest.
2. The Romans did it, being approved by Pontius Pilate.
3. The devil did it, having engineered the betrayal by Judas Iscariot.
4. God did it, having planned it from the foundation of the world.
5. We all did it, having put Him on the cross owing to our sins.

I saw my sins His blood had spilt,
And helped to nail Him there.

—John Newton (1725–1807)

When Peter said, "You killed the author of life," he was addressing Jews generally (Acts 3:15). And yet, as noted above, Paul's comment later on shows that Satan was the architect of Jesus' death. He spoke of God's wisdom, "a mystery that had been hidden and that God destined for our glory before time began." It turns out that part of this hidden wisdom was allowing darkness to reign, whereby Satan directed the scenario of Jesus' arrest, trial, and crucifixion.

> None of the rulers of this age understood it, for if they had, they would not have crucified the Lord of glory.
>
> —1 Corinthians 2:8

Incidents That Would Have Delighted Satan

Imagine, then, what was possibly going on in Satan's mind during the crucifixion and the events that led to it. The following must have given Satan a measure of pleasure.

- Satan prompting Judas to betray Jesus (John 13:2)
- Satan entering Judas (John 13:27)
- Jesus sweating drops of blood in Gethsemane (Luke 22:44)
- Judas betraying Jesus with a kiss (Luke 22:48)
- The chief priests and officers arresting Jesus (Luke 22:52)
- Jesus before the Sanhedrin and high priest (Matt. 26:57–67; John 18:19–24)
- All His disciples deserting Him and fleeing (Matt. 26:56; Mark 14:50)
- Peter denying Jesus (Luke 22:54–62; John 18:17, 25–27)
- The guards and later the soldiers mocking Jesus (Luke 22:63–65; Mark 15:16–20)

- Judas hanging himself (Matt. 27:1–5)
- Jesus before Pilate (Luke 23:1–6)
- Jesus before Herod (Luke 23:7–10)
- Jesus before Pilate again (Luke 23:11–22; John 18:28–19:16)
- Pilate agreeing to have Jesus crucified (Luke 23:24–25)
- The crucifixion (John 19:18; Luke 23:33)
- The chief priests and teachers of the law mocking Jesus (Mark 15:31–32)
- Jesus' death (Luke 23:46; John 19:30)

What would have delighted Satan *most* was Jesus' actual death. That gave him cause for celebration. As some preachers have attempted to describe this moment—as I have—it is when Satan popped champagne corks in hell and exclaimed with his demons, "We did it! We did it! We did it! He's dead. He's gone. We won!"

Incidents That Might Have Given Satan Pause

These things said, there were things happening while Jesus was hanging on the cross that could have disturbed Satan. I refer to four supernatural events—all of which defy a natural explanation:

- Darkness came over all the land—from noon until three o'clock (Matt. 27:45; Mark 15:33; Luke 23:44)
- The curtain of the temple was torn in two from top to bottom (Matt. 27:51; Luke 23:45)
- The earthquake (Matt. 27:51)

- The bodies of many saints were raised to life (Matt. 27:52–53)

Satan may not have noticed these happenings. He may have been so pleased that Jesus was actually dead that nothing else would have fazed him. These events may appear to be natural at first. For example, some think the darkness over the land was an eclipse of the sun. Not true.

1. Darkness

The darkness that covered the land was supernatural. It was the *shekinah* glory. It was a seal of the Holy Spirit on the atonement of Jesus. A seal on His blood.

When the Lord first spoke to Moses about the Day of Atonement (*Yom Kippur*), He promised to "appear in the cloud over the atonement" (Lev. 16:2). When darkness covered the earth from noon until 3:00 p.m. on Good Friday, *it was that cloud.* We know that cloud was "dark" because Solomon observed it. Immediately after the temple of Solomon was finished, the ark of the covenant was brought into the temple. It was a great celebration. One hundred twenty priests sounded trumpets. "The trumpeters and musicians joined in unison to give praise and thanks to the LORD. Accompanied by trumpets, cymbals and other instruments, the singers raised their voices in praise to the LORD and sang: 'He is good; his love endures forever'" (2 Chron. 5:11–13).

> Then the temple of the LORD was filled with the cloud, and the priests could not perform their service because of the cloud, for the glory of the LORD filled the temple of God. Then Solomon said, "The LORD has said that he would dwell *in a dark cloud*; I have built a magnificent temple for you, a place for you to dwell forever."
>
> —2 CHRONICLES 5:13–6:2, EMPHASIS ADDED

The darkness therefore that covered the whole land from the sixth to the ninth hour was that same dark cloud—the glory of the Lord—that Solomon spoke of, which came into the temple after the ark of the covenant was brought in.

Not that the devil would have noticed this. He would only be delighting in what he thought was the demise of his archenemy—Jesus Christ.

2. The curtain of the temple

The curtain being torn from top to bottom was another seal of the Most High on the atonement of Jesus' death on the cross. That curtain separated the Holy Place from the Most Holy Place. Moses was specifically told that his brother Aaron was not to enter the Most Holy Place whenever he chose. He must not enter "into the Most Holy Place behind the curtain in front of the atonement cover on the ark, or else he will die" (Lev. 16:2).

That curtain had been hanging in the temple for years and, as James Stewart said, "It looked as if it might hang there forever."[2] But at the precise moment Jesus breathed His last breath, that curtain was torn in two "from top to bottom"—showing the tear originated from above; no human being could have done that. It was an undoubted seal of God upon the atonement of Jesus Christ, further showing that you and I may enter into the very presence of God "by the blood of Jesus" (Heb. 10:19).

3. The earthquake

The *timing* of the earthquake shows it was supernatural. Earthquakes are generally a natural phenomenon. But the earthquake transpiring at the precise moment Jesus breathed His last breath—being inserted by Matthew—was to show the seal of the Creator God upon the death of Jesus. In other words, His death was more than a crucifixion; it was atonement. All creation bows to the Lord Jesus Christ.

4. The saints raised to life

The bodies of certain saints known to be dead and raised to life was obviously a supernatural event. It was a seal of God on the shed blood of Jesus, which guaranteed eternal life and our own resurrection from the dead. Even before Jesus' actual resurrection, then, God chose certain holy people in Jerusalem known to have died that were recognizable. People knew they had died. But they suddenly appeared. This is so amazing that it is a mystery that Matthew did not say more. But one sentence was enough; it shows that the blood of Jesus "might break the power of him who holds the power of death—that is, the devil—and free those who all their lives were held in slavery by their fear of death" (Heb. 2:14–15).

"You killed the author of life," said Peter, "but God raised him from the dead" (Acts 3:15)—the devil's worst nightmare. Satan did not anticipate this or, as we have been saying, he would not have crucified the Lord of glory (1 Cor. 2:8).

Satan had no idea what was going on. What he was thinking between the moment of Jesus' death and resurrection on Easter morning is of course speculation. But one thing is certain; he did not anticipate Jesus' resurrection from the dead! Whatever champagne party that may have taken place in hell on Good Friday came to an abrupt end on Easter morning. What became the greatest news of all time for the human race was the worst news for Satan. It was infallible proof that there would be the final resurrection of the dead and infallible proof of Satan's eventual doom.

Pentecost

Fifty days following the crucifixion of Jesus came the day of Pentecost—the commemoration of the giving of the Law at Mount Sinai. It showed that all was going according to plan—God's plan. The falling of the Holy Spirit empowered the early disciples, numbering 120. Peter's anointed sermon resulted in 3,000 people converted. The devil's worst nightmare—the resurrection of Jesus—was succeeded by another nightmare: the empowering presence of the Holy Spirit.

Later on, when the small church in Jerusalem needed a platform, Peter healed a man who had never walked (Acts 3:1–10). This gave the disciples an opportunity to address those who lived in Jerusalem. Most of those converted on the day of Pentecost were from outside Jerusalem. But the miracle of healing caused Jerusalem Jews to listen to Peter after the undoubted miracle: "You killed the author of life, but God raised him from the dead" (Acts 3:15). Thousands more were converted (Acts 4:4).

Things were happening so fast that Satan never caught up with the church's early success. The best the devil could do was to move into the pride and greed of Ananias and Sapphira. After that came the jealousy that divided the Greek Jews from the Hebrew Jews. Satan exploited this, but filling Ananias and Sapphira's hearts did not thwart the growth of the early church. There was so much power of the Holy Spirit present that people just hoped to get into Peter's shadow in order to get healed (Acts 5:15).

The Conversion of Saul of Tarsus

Saul of Tarsus chasing after Christians in order to destroy them and stop the growth of the Christian faith fit nicely into Satan's plan. The last thing the devil would want—or expect—was that his number one agent on planet earth would be converted. But it happened. "Thy people shall be willing in the day of thy power" (Ps. 110:3, KJV). Saul of Tarsus willingly submitted to the power of the Spirit: "What shall I do, Lord?" (Acts 22:10). From that moment Saul of Tarsus made a one-hundred-eighty-degree turn and became as zealous for Jesus Christ as he had been to destroy His followers. Immediately Paul began preaching! "At once he began to preach in the synagogues that Jesus is the Son of God"

(Acts 9:20). There is no way to gauge the thinking process of Satan, but it is possible that Saul's conversion was the devil's worst nightmare next to Jesus' resurrection.

One thing is certain: Paul was famous in hell. It did not take long for him to get known in hell. Shortly after his conversion, Paul entered into a preparation period that lasted perhaps fourteen years (Gal. 1:18–2:1). Although Paul started preaching immediately after his conversion, God set him aside for preparation. God made sure Paul did not succeed until he was ready. Preparation is essential to the refinement of one's anointing. Charles Spurgeon said that if he knew he would have twenty-five years left to live, he would spend twenty of it in preparation. Joseph waited more than twenty years before his dreams were fulfilled. David was anointed by the Spirit in power (1 Sam. 16:13) but did not wear the crown for another twenty years. Paul was partly prepared by his being tutored by the famous Gamaliel (Acts 22:3), but he needed time to do a lot of unlearning and grasp how the Law fit into his new faith. In addition to intellectual preparation, Paul was anointed to see people healed and was at home with the miraculous as well as with the word (Rom. 15:19; 1 Thess. 1:5). Above all, Paul was an evangelist. He lived to preach the gospel. He would end up writing virtually two-thirds of the New Testament. No wonder, then, that the demon would say, "Paul I know about" (Acts 19:15).

I repeat the question: Does the demonic world know about you and me?

The Christian faith was spreading fast before Saul became the apostle Paul. Mind you, some in the early church were suspicious of Paul. I'm not sure how many welcomed him warmly! It took Barnabas—who was trusted by the Jews—to make all feel better about Paul (Acts 9:27). In any case, the conclusion was reached by the early church leaders that Peter would preach to the Jews, and Paul to the Gentiles (Gal. 2:7).

Satan would realize too that if God's power could turn a Saul of Tarsus around, God could do it again and again. Satan is called the "god of this age" and does all he can do to keep people blind from the knowledge of the glory of God in Christ (2 Cor. 4:4).

This is a great encouragement. As we seek to win the lost to Christ—whether they be rich or famous, poor or unknown—the gospel is the power of God for salvation. No case is too difficult for Him. That is why Paul said he was unashamed of the gospel (Rom. 1:16). God is on our side. We should not be surprised that God will save the most difficult case imaginable! I expect that in these last days God will raise up a thousand Sauls of Tarsus—whether they be Harvard professors, movie stars, well-known atheists, mafia members, sports heroes, the superrich, or politicians—to confound Satan and the world. Nothing is impossible with God.

Although the Christian faith was growing all over Judea and Samaria, it was Paul who gave the early church its greatest impetus. Paul and Barnabas worked together for a while, ministering in Cyprus (Acts 13:4–12), in Pisidian Antioch (vv. 13–52), in Iconium (Acts 14:1–7), in Lystra and Derbe (vv. 8–21). Paul and Barnabas had a sharp disagreement regarding the reliability of Mark (Acts 15:36–39), and Paul decided to work with Silas. They traveled through the region of Phyrgia and Galatia (Acts 16:6), Macedonia (v. 12), Philippi (v. 12), and Thessalonica (Acts 17:1–9). By the time they came to Thessalonica, their reputation preceded them. The Jews in Thessalonica were jealous of Paul and Silas and shouted: "These men who have caused trouble all over the world have now come here" (Acts 17:5–6).

When we cause trouble like that we should be thankful. It may be we have been promoted to a great class of people. Ahab called Elijah, God's "troubler of Israel" (1 Kings 18:17). What a compliment!

The irony is, men like Peter, Barnabas, Silas, and Paul became famous in the world. That was not their intent, nor did this matter to them. But that is the way it turned out. The main thing, however, is that they became famous in hell.

Satan could not stop this phenomenal growth in the ancient Mediterranean world. Truly the gates of Hades could not prevail against the church (Matt. 16:18). "All those the Father gives me will come to me," said Jesus (John 6:37).

To be Satan's greatest nightmare! Oh how we might wish for this!

> Go, labor on: spend, and be spent,
> Thy joy to do the Father's will;
> It is the way the Master went;
> Should not the servant tread it still?
>
> Go, labor on! 'Tis not for naught
> Thine earthly loss is heav'nly gain;
> Men heed thee, love thee, praise thee not;
> The Master praises: what are men?[3]
>
> —Horatius Bonar (1808–1889)

Chapter 12

QUALIFICATIONS FOR FAME IN HELL

When they saw the courage of Peter and
John and realized they were unschooled,
ordinary men, they were astonished and they
took note that these men had been with Jesus.

—Acts 4:13

We began this book quoting Acts 4:13, and so we end with it in this our final chapter.

It is important to realize that you do not have to be famous on earth to be famous in hell. You don't have to be the pope, the archbishop of Canterbury, or Billy Graham to be famous in hell. The qualification for being famous in hell comes down to two things:

1. Having boldness and courage
2. You have been with Jesus

Satan trembles, when he sees the weakest saint upon his knees.[1]

—William Cowper (1731–1800)

We must however make a distinction between being known in hell and being famous in hell. You may recall that when the evil spirit called out, "Jesus I know [*ginōskō*], and I know about Paul [*epistamai*]" (Acts 19:15), the demon does not say that Jesus and Paul were famous in hell. But I am sure of this: Jesus and Paul were famous in hell.

Paul was famous in Ephesus by the time the extraordinary episode with the sons of Sceva took place. These sons of a Jewish chief priest were very much aware of Paul and the gospel he preached. The sons commanded the demon to come out "in the name of Jesus, whom Paul preaches." This also shows that the sons of Sceva were very aware of the *content* of Paul's preaching. In a word, *Paul preached Jesus*. This tallies with Paul's own words: "I resolved to know nothing while I was with you except Jesus Christ and him crucified" (1 Cor. 2:2). (I would hope the world would describe my preaching the same way.)

What then is the distinction between being known in hell and being famous in hell? First, *every* Christian is known in hell. After all, when one crosses over from "death to life" (John 5:24) the world of Tartarus would have taken notice! They lost one of their own! Indeed, such a person has been turned "from darkness to light, and from the power of Satan to God" (Acts 26:18). When a person comes to Christ in faith, he or she gets a new enemy—the devil. That being true, Satan knows about every person who has sided with his archenemy, Jesus Christ. All Christians are known in hell.

These things said, not every Christian's name would be cited as Paul's name was. The sons of Sceva's liturgy invoked Paul's very name. Paul making a stir in Ephesus made him known to all, including the sons of Sceva. Paul had at first gone into the synagogue in Ephesus and spoke "boldly" there for three months, "arguing persuasively about the kingdom of God" (Acts 19:8). However, "some of them became obstinate; they refused to believe and publicly maligned the Way. So Paul left them" (v. 9). They then went to the lecture hall of Tyrannus as their new venue. They had daily discussions there for two years, so that "*all the Jews and Greeks* who lived in the providence of Asia heard the word of the Lord" (v. 10, emphasis added). This shows that Paul was famous in Ephesus. Not only that, but "God did extraordinary miracles through Paul, so that even handkerchiefs and aprons that had *touched him* were taken to the sick, and their illnesses were cured and the *evil spirits* left them" (vv. 11–12, emphasis added).

That evil spirits were exorcised from people through Paul's ministry shows that Paul would have been *very* known in hell. He would have been a threat to the satanic world big time. It is one thing to be known in hell because you are a Christian, but to have demonic spirits exorcised shows that you are much more than merely known. In a word, Paul was famous in hell. Not all Christians are famous in hell. It is not common that a person has power entrusted to him by God that he sees people healed *and* delivered—even by *handkerchiefs* that touched his very *body*!

And yet *any* Christian may aspire to be famous in hell. If Satan trembles when he sees the weakest saints upon their knees, such a person of prayer may qualify for fame in hell. A pursuit like that is initiated by *being with Jesus*. When you spend time in prayer, you spend time with Jesus. Being with Jesus gives you confidence. Being with Jesus will give you a desire to walk in all the light He gives you (1 John 1:7). Walking in the light leads to obedience to the Word—the Bible—and the Holy Spirit. Focusing on the Word enables you to display the "fruit of the Spirit" (Gal. 5:22–25). Openness to the Holy Spirit will cause you to desire eagerly the "greater gifts" of the Spirit (1 Cor. 12:31).

Being with Jesus therefore leads to courage. Being in His presence gives you boldness. Being unashamed. "For the Spirit God gave us does not make us timid, but gives us power, love and self-discipline" (2 Tim. 1:7).

You are not required to be famous on earth to be famous in hell. You are not required to be an apostle to be famous in hell. You are not required to be rich, old, brilliant, a seasoned saint, or educated to be famous in hell. It is a level playing ground. Being with Jesus is required. Furthermore, if your heart is warmed as you read these lines, it tells me God is on your case and is giving you a special invitation to be famous in hell.

But there is nothing glamorous in this venture. Be prepared to be rejected, misunderstood, laughed at, and vilified. It is part of the package. To be the devil's worst nightmare comes with a cost—maintaining transparent integrity, sexual purity, and sacrificing your pride. Though it cost you "all you have" (Prov. 4:7), apply now to be famous in hell. Applications are being accepted at the throne of grace. Come with confidence to King Jesus and ask for mercy that you will receive grace in the time of need (Heb. 4:16).

I have no way of knowing what proportion of Christians are famous in hell. But possibly more than we might think. The invitation is certainly open to all.

Those people of faith described in Hebrews 11 were not only known in hell but famous in hell. But they were largely unknown on earth—at first—in their own day. They achieved greatness by faith. Not by intelligence. Or education. Or being well connected. It was by faith—believing God. Believing what He said. Believing His Word. Many of these consequently turned the world upside down in their own day.

My friend Rolfe Barnard (1904–1969) used to say, "One of these days someone is going to come along, read the Bible and believe it—and put the rest of us to shame."

British readers will know about Jennifer Rees Larcombe, who has a writing and speaking ministry in England. In 1982 she was stricken with a virus called encephalitis. She was immediately disabled through damage to her central nervous system. She was confined to a wheelchair while keeping up a speaking ministry all over England. I remember talking with her in Bristol as she sat in a wheelchair. During those eight years she was prayed for many times. Many people—including those who had a ministry in healing—hoped to be the one who would pray for her and she be healed. After she spoke in an event in 1990, a young lady who had been a Christian for three weeks asked Jennifer if she could pray for her. Of course. An utter surprise followed. Jennifer was instantly healed. She carried her wheelchair home and cooked supper that evening! God did not use a high-profile faith healer, but a young lady who had been converted three weeks before.

The writer of the letter to the Hebrews lists men and women who are famous to us, but were by and large unknown on earth in their own generation. No doubt people like Moses were famous, and many of those he lists were well known to God's covenant people when they were alive—Joseph, Samuel, and David. But the writer of Hebrews proceeds to mention nameless, unknown people:

> There were others who were tortured, refusing to be released so that they might gain an even better resurrection. Some faced jeers and flogging, and even chains and imprisonment. They were put to death by stoning; they were sawed in two; they were killed by the sword. They went about in sheepskins and goatskins, destitute, persecuted and mistreated—the world was not worthy of them. They wandered in deserts and mountains, living in caves and holes in the ground.
>
> —Hebrews 11:35–38

Note that it says "the world was not worthy of them." But the world would not agree! "Men...praise thee not," wrote Horatius Bonar (quoted previously), but "the Master praises: what are men?" That line always comes close to bringing me to tears. What a comparison: praise from Jesus *vis-à-vis* praise of men. What are men? One thing you can be assured of: the fear of man is a snare (Prov. 29:25). The praise of men can be so misleading.

To become famous in hell you must be willing to abandon any craving of fame on the earth. If you are only wanting to be famous on the earth, chances are you will forfeit an opportunity to be famous in hell.

In any case, you don't have to be an apostle Paul to be famous in hell. However, it seems fitting nonetheless to see what Paul himself was truly like. Even if you manage to become like Paul, it does not follow that you will do what he did—or become famous in hell. But it would not be surprising if God asks you and me to do what it takes to be His transparent instrument—"useful to the Master and prepared to do any good work" (2 Tim. 2:21). Everyone who confesses the name of the Lord must "turn away from wickedness" (v. 19).

> In a large house there are articles not only of gold and silver, but also of wood and clay; some are for special purposes and some for common use. Those who cleanse themselves from the latter will be instruments for special purposes, made holy, useful to the Master and prepared to do any good work.
>
> —2 Timothy 2:20–21

The gifts and calling of God are without repentance; they are irrevocable (Rom. 11:29). That said, it should not be surprising when God uses less than perfect vessels to accomplish His purpose. "We have this treasure in jars of clay to show that this all-surpassing power is from God and not from us" (2 Cor. 4:7). Moreover, we must never forget that God said to Moses, "I will have mercy on whom I have mercy" (Exod. 33:19; Rom. 9:15). In a word, God can use anybody He chooses. God is sovereign.

However, you and I should make it our aim to be God's

"instruments for special purposes, made holy, useful to the Master and prepared to do any good work" (2 Tim. 2:21). With this in mind, I want us to take a good look at the man Paul. I would have thought it presumptuous for us to aspire to be famous in hell if we did not do all in our power and strength to be like he was. After all he did say that he was an "example" or "pattern" (KJV) for those who believe on Christ (1 Tim. 1:16). He even said, "Follow my example, as I follow the example of Christ" (1 Cor. 11:1).

There is no need for me to show why Jesus was famous in hell. But I now list reasons for knowing Paul was famous in hell.

Five Things About Paul

1. He was primarily a soul winner.

Some of us tend to see in Paul what we want to see. I might see him as a theologian. Another might see him as a missionary. Or pastor. Or an apostle. Or preacher. Or a man very like Jesus. All these would be true.

But I have come to the conclusion in my old age that Paul was primarily and uppermost an evangelist. "I am not ashamed of the gospel, because it is the power of God that brings salvation to everyone who believes: first to the Jew, then to the Gentile" (Rom. 1:16). "It has always been my ambition to preach the gospel where Christ was not known, so that I would not be building on someone else's foundation" (Rom. 15:20). "I have become all things to all people so that by all possible means *I might save some*" (1 Cor. 9:22, emphasis added)—such language coming from a man who believed in sovereign grace!

Paul lived to see people saved. In his final letter he cautioned Timothy: "Do the work of an evangelist" (2 Tim. 4:5). When he had time to spare in Athens because Silas and Timothy were held up, what did Paul do? He went to the marketplace daily to witness to those "who happened to be there" (Acts 17:17).

This reminds me of Bob George, one of our deacons at Westminster Chapel. In my early days there I asked the congregation: "How many of you have never led a soul to Jesus Christ?"

Mr. George told me later: "Those words struck me rigid. I suddenly realized, 'Here I am sixty years old, and I have never led a single soul to the Lord.'" But when we began our Pilot Light ministry a few years later, Mr. George was the first to join us on the streets to witness for Christ. He never missed a Saturday, and he rarely had a Saturday in which he did not lead someone to pray to receive Christ. Always having a smile on his face, his happiest moment was when he had just led a person to Jesus. I used to say to Louise, "When Mr. George leads a person to the Lord, he looks like the cat that swallowed the canary." The last time I talked with him before he died, when he was eighty years old, he had led more than five hundred souls to pray to receive Christ. One of them went into the Anglican ministry.

Bob George was famous in hell.

Like his father, Malcolm George—a man born with muscular dystrophy, who, although mentally sharp, could never speak clearly and walked with a severe limp all his life—I believe also became famous in hell.

He was an original Pilot Light. When I announced that we would begin witnessing on the streets of Victoria, calling ourselves Pilot Lights, Bob George and his son, Malcolm, were among the original six to show up.

There was a day when Malcolm was extremely discouraged over what he perceived as being a failure as a street witness. "I am just a waste of space," he said to Louise after a Sunday night service. He was aware that almost nobody understood him, but for some reason Louise could always understand him.

"Think of all the tracts you have given out in all those many languages," Louise said to Malcolm, trying so hard to encourage him, adding, "You will find out in heaven."

"No. I am just a waste of space," he kept saying.

But at that precise moment a French lady came into the back hall following the Sunday night service. She came in with one of our members, Marta Jenks, who spoke French. She came looking for the man who gave her a tract the Saturday before. She suddenly shouted in French, "There he is! That is the man who gave me a tract in French yesterday."

It was Malcolm. She ran to him and hugged him. She had been converted through reading the tract. The next time she was in London she came to Westminster Chapel—and sat with Malcolm. Words cannot describe the look on his face the whole time she sat with him.

I believe Malcolm George did the work of an evangelist and became famous in hell.

2. Paul was not afraid to die.

He looked forward to seeing Christ when he died. He struggled to know which was better—to die and be with the Lord—or remain. He said, "To live is Christ and to die is gain" (Phil. 1:21). He stated to the elders of the church at Ephesus: "I consider my life *worth nothing* to me" (Acts 20:24, emphasis added). Those who overcame by the blood of the Lamb and by the word of their testimony "did not love their lives so much as to shrink from death" (Rev. 12:11).

Josef Tson used to say to me, "The most dangerous person in the world is a person not afraid to die." Clear examples of this are suicide bombers in the Middle East, and more recently in New York City and other American cities. They are unafraid to die and are therefore the most dangerous people in the world. What motivates them, however, is a false hope of being given seventy-two virgins when they die. Our hope is knowing that Jesus died on the cross for our sins; that His blood bought us a home in heaven. As a consequence of this factual truth, we know where we will go when we die!

Billy Graham told a funny story about Albert Einstein. On a train Einstein lost his ticket. When the conductor came to receive tickets, Einstein got down on the floor, looking for his ticket. The conductor said, "Dr. Einstein, don't worry, I know who you are." Einstein replied: "I too know who I am. What I don't know is where I'm going." Then Billy Graham commented: "I not only know who I am, I also know where I'm going."[2]

Paul was a dangerous man! He was fearless. unashamed of the gospel. He did not care what it took to follow Christ. He had no fear of death.

3. He refused to vindicate himself.

One of Paul's deepest pains was having his own converts turn against him and question his integrity. A group of Jews who called themselves Christians followed Paul wherever he went—only to undermine his integrity and theology. Paul said that Gentile Christians don't need to be circumcised; these men—now known as Judaizers—said that Gentile Christians must be circumcised. These men were not soul winners; they only fished in the Christian pond. They lived to undermine Paul and managed to get Paul's own converts to doubt him. This gave him great pain. If I had to choose what I think was Paul's "thorn in the flesh" (2 Cor. 12:7, KJV) I would say these Judaizers. But Paul was willing to let God vindicate him.

Among those converts who questioned his theology and integrity were some of those in Corinth. Paul said to them:

> I care very little if I am judged by you or by any human court; indeed, I do not even judge myself. My conscience is clear, but that does not make me innocent. It is the Lord who judges me. Therefore judge nothing before the appointed time; wait until the Lord comes. He will bring

> to light what is hidden in darkness and will expose the motives of the heart. At that time each will receive their praise from God.
>
> —1 Corinthians 4:3–5

When we succumb to the need to vindicate ourselves, it can remove our being a threat to Satan. Those who are famous in hell will likely be those who follow Paul. The greatest liberty is having nothing to prove. Paul was very willing for people to think what they chose to think, knowing that the truth will come out at the judgment seat of Christ.

4. A reward at the judgment seat of Christ was important to him.

All who pass from death to life by the power of the Holy Spirit will be in heaven one day. That is a given. Once saved, always saved. But sadly not all Christians will receive a reward at the judgment seat of Christ. Some will be saved by fire—"escaping through the flames" (1 Cor. 3:15). I don't know what that reward is. If it is hearing from the lips of Jesus Himself, "Well done," that is enough for me.

And yet sadly there are those who say, "I don't care if I don't receive a reward at the judgment seat of Christ, I just want to make it to heaven." My reply: You won't feel that way then. What is more, it is no great sign of spiritual maturity to be indifferent about a reward at the judgment seat of Christ. The fact that it was so important to Paul convinces me it should be important to every Christian. When Paul wrote 1 Corinthians about AD 55, he could not guarantee that he himself would receive this reward:

> Do you not know that in a race all the runners run, but only one gets the prize? Run in such a way as to get the prize. Everyone who competes in the games goes into strict training. They do it to get a crown that will not last, but we

> do it that will get a crown that will last forever. Therefore I do not run like someone running aimlessly; I do not fight like a boxer beating the air. No, I strike a blow to my body and make it my slave so that after I have preached to others, I myself will not be disqualified for the prize.
>
> —1 Corinthians 9:24–27

But when Paul wrote ten years later, he was convinced he would get the prize, crown, or reward.

> For I am already being poured out like a drink offering, and the time for my departure is near. I have fought the good fight, I have finished the race, I have kept the faith. Now there is in store for me the crown of righteousness, which the Lord, the righteous Judge, will award to me on that day—not only to me, but also to all who have longed for his appearing.
>
> —2 Timothy 4:6–8

If we take our cue from Paul, we too will want to receive a reward at the judgment seat of Christ (2 Cor. 5:10). Those who have their eyes on this will be those who want their lives to be God honoring. Such people qualify for fame in hell.

5. His earthly accomplishments meant nothing to him.

Paul had an impressive pedigree.

> Circumcised on the eighth day, of the people of Israel, of the tribe of Benjamin, a Hebrew of Hebrews; in regard to the law, a Pharisee; as for zeal, persecuting the church; as for righteousness based on the law, faultless. But whatever were gains to me I now consider loss for the sake of Christ. What is more, I consider everything a loss because of the surpassing worth of knowing Christ Jesus my Lord, for whose sake I have lost all things. I consider them garbage, that I may gain Christ and be found in him, not having

> a righteousness of my own that comes from the law, but that which is through faith in Christ—the righteousness that comes from God on the basis of faith. I want to know Christ—yes, to know the power of his resurrection and participation in his sufferings, becoming like him in his death, and so, somehow, attaining to the resurrection from the dead.
>
> —Philippians 3:5–11

There was a time when Paul's background, pedigree, and accomplishments were very important to him. But he now regarded all that as "loss" for the sake of Christ. "Rubbish." What became utterly important to him was "knowing Christ." "But wait a minute, Paul," we might say. "We thought you knew the Lord!" He would reply: "Oh yes, I do know Him. But not like I want to know Him." Paul wanted to explore the surpassing greatness of just knowing Jesus Christ and not reflecting on any of his own past accomplishments.

Paul kept his eyes on Jesus. Of course he was aware of his accomplishments. He was not blind to his past, nor had he lost his memory. But now he was transfixed on the person of Jesus Christ—so much so that he aspired to suffer as Jesus did. Jesus had a false trial and did not complain. Jesus suffered torture and did not complain. Like a lamb before its shearers is dumb so Jesus "did not open his mouth" (Isa. 53:7). He was mocked but did not retort. That is what Paul means by saying he wanted to be like Jesus in His death.

Years ago I used to listen to an old spiritual sung by the famous African American Marian Anderson (1897–1993). I still google her from time to time just to hear her sing this old spiritual:

> They crucified my Lord, and He never said a mumbalin'
> word;

They crucified my Lord, and He never said a mumbalin'
word.
Not a word, not a word, not a word.

He bowed His head and died, but He never said a
mumbalin' word;
He bowed His head and died, but He never said a
mumbalin' word.
Not a word, not a word, not a word.[3]

That is what Paul meant by wanting to know Christ and be like Him in His death.

Any person who reaches that state of desiring God will likely be famous in hell. A person like that is a threat to Satan's interests. Hell has their number.

CONCLUSION

I HAVE WRITTEN THIS book with the hope that you would aspire to be popular in heaven and famous in hell. It is my own wish. I want it to be yours too. I want my life to be a threat to Satan.

> Some want to live within the sound
> Of church or chapel bell;
> I want to run a rescue shop,
> Within a yard of hell.[1]
>
> —C. T. STUDD

The danger however with such an ambition is always that we will take ourselves too seriously and become self-righteous. God hates this. Self-righteousness disqualifies us from being popular in heaven and famous in hell. This is why we must make every effort not to let our right hand know what our left hand is doing. We must do this when it comes to giving, fasting, and praying (Matt. 6:1–8, 16–18) but also with any other sense of spiritual accomplishment—whether walking in the light, dignifying trials, or demonstrating total forgiveness.

I believe we can know we are popular in heaven. God wants us to know this. But only with deepest humility, being conscious of our sinfulness and an ever-lurking potential to mess up.

I am less sure we can know we are famous in hell. We have seen that we can be known in hell without being famous in hell. The devil himself might tempt you and me to assume that we are famous in hell—so we will take ourselves too seriously. Those who take themselves very seriously are a minimal threat to the powers of darkness.

The only remedy against self-righteousness is a steadfast gaze on the face of Jesus (Heb. 12:2)—refusing to take our eyes off Him for a second.

As we close our time together, I am now going to do something I have not done in any of the other books I have written. I am going to repeat word for word a paragraph that comes from the opening chapter. I do so because I believe that try as I might I will not be able to capture in better words the heart—and the vital importance—of what I have been sharing with you.

My dear reader, life is short. The things that grasp our attention now will one day seem like mere trinkets. Every day we breathe in and out—in and out—thousands of times a day. There is a day fixed, that unless Jesus comes first, you and I will only breathe *out*. No amount of money, power, or prestige can alter the date that we each have with death. And at that moment the only thing that will matter is whether we have known Christ and served Him well—that our lives have made a difference. In short: that we are popular in heaven—and famous in hell.

With all my heart I pray that both you and I may know that double blessing.

I suggest you pray this prayer:

> *Lord Jesus, I believe You have a purpose in bringing this book to me. Help me to grasp what is in it that brings honor and glory to Your name. Give me grace to apply these truths in my life. I want to be popular with You. And if You will enable me, to be famous in hell. Help me to keep my eyes focused on You. May my life bring great honor and glory to Your name. Amen.*

May the grace of our Lord Jesus Christ, the love and tender mercy of God the Father, and the fellowship, grace, and peace together with the sprinkling of the blood of Jesus by the Holy Spirit be with you and *stay* with you now and evermore. Amen.

NOTES

Chapter 2
The Fleeting Privilege of Faith

1. A video with Oprah Winfrey articulating this view may be viewed at https://www.youtube.com/watch?v=n2SrZJlPnjk.

Chapter 3
Disappointed—But Still Believing

1. John Calvin, *Calvin's Commentaries*, Acts 7, BibleHub.com, accessed March 20, 2018, http://biblehub.com/commentaries/calvin/acts/7.htm.
2. R. T. Kendall, *All's Well That Ends Well* (London: Paternoster, 2005).
3. R. T. Kendall, *God Meant It for Good* (Fort Mill, SC: MorningStar Publications, 2008).
4. R. T. Kendall, *Believing God* (Fort Mill, SC: MorningStar Publications, 2003).
5. R. T. Kendall, *The Anointing* (Lake Mary, FL: Charisma House, 2003).
6. R. T. Kendall, *A Man After God's Own Heart* (United Kingdom: Christian Focus, 2001).
7. Robert Frost, *The Poetry of Robert Frost: The Collected Poems, Complete and Unabridged*, ed. Edward Connery Lathem (New York: Macmillan, 2002), 105.

Chapter 4
Popularity in Heaven: An Earthly Choice

1. Dale Carnegie, *How to Win Friends and Influence People* (New York: Simon & Schuster, 1981).
2. Philip D. W. Krey and Peter D. S. Krey, ed. and trans., *Luther's Spirituality* (New York: Paulist Press, 2007), xxvii.
3. Sir Julian Huxley, cited on *The Merv Griffin Show*, 1969, Narkive Newsgroup Archive, accessed May 29, 2018, http://uk.philosophy.atheism.narkive.com/BSqLXH3l/why-do-u-suppose-evolutionist-sir-julian-huxley-would-say-this.
4. R. T. Kendall, *Tithing* (Grand Rapids, MI: Zondervan, 1983).

5. "C. T. Studd Quotes," Goodreads Inc., accessed April 13, 2018, https://www.goodreads.com/quotes/715176-if-jesus-christ-be-god-and-died-for-me-then.
6. Winston Churchill, "Never Give In," The International Churchill Society, accessed April 13, 2018, https://winstonchurchill.org/resources/speeches/1941-1945-war-leader/never-give-in-harrow-school/.

Chapter 5
The Honor and Praise of God

1. R. T. Kendall and David Rosen, *The Christian and the Pharisee* (London: Hodder & Stoughton LTD, 2006).
2. R. T. Kendall, *Why Jesus Died* (Oxford: Monarch Books, 2011).
3. R. T. Kendall, *Are You Stone Deaf to the Spirit or Rediscovering God?* (United Kingdom: Christian Focus, 2001).
4. "Mr. Frank Jenner; the George Street Evangelist," June 7, 2013, https://www.christianstogether.net/Articles/82079/Christians_Together_in/Christian_Life/Reaching_Out/Mr_Jenner_and/Mr_Frank_Jenner.aspx.
5. Phil Ryken, "The Man From George Street, Part 9," December 23, 2006, http://www.reformation21.org/blog/2006/12/the-man-from-george-street-par.php.
6. "Miracle on George Street," YouTube video, posted by LordShadrach, May 9, 2009, https://www.youtube.com/watch?v=bvnmidVF9Xg&feature=youtu.be.
7. "Miracle on George Street," YouTube video.

Chapter 6
What Is Unpopular in Heaven?

1. R. T. Kendall, *Holy Fire* (Lake Mary, FL: Charisma House, 2014).
2. "Abortions This Year," Worldometers.info, accessed May 30, 2018, http://www.worldometers.info/abortions/.
3. "Abortion Statistics for England and Wales: See the Latest Breakdown," Guardian News and Media Limited, accessed May 30, 2018, https://www.theguardian.com/news/datablog/2011/may/24/abortion-statistics-england-wales.
4. "Internet Pornography by the Numbers; a Significant Threat to Society," Webroot Inc., accessed May 30, 2018, https://www

.webroot.com/us/en/resources/tips-articles/internet -pornography-by-the-numbers.

5. "Internet Pornography by the Numbers; a Significant Threat to Society," Webroot Inc.
6. "Internet Pornography by the Numbers; a Significant Threat to Society," Webroot Inc.
7. "Internet Pornography by the Numbers; a Significant Threat to Society," Webroot Inc.
8. Marcus Jones, "42% of UK Christian Men Admit 'Porn Addiction,'" Premier, January 16, 2015, https://www.premier.org.uk /News/UK/42-of-UK-Christian-men-admit-porn-addiction.
9. Jones, "42% of UK Christian Men Admit 'Porn Addiction.'"
10. Jones, "42% of UK Christian Men Admit 'Porn Addiction.'"
11. Meredith Somers, "More Than Half of Christian Men Admit to Watching Pornography," *Washington Times*, August 24, 2014, https://www.washingtontimes.com/news/2014/aug/24/more-than-half-of-christian-men-admit-to-watching-/.
12. R. T. Kendall, *Total Forgiveness* (Lake Mary, FL: Charisma House, 2007).
13. R. T. Kendall, *Whatever Happened to the Gospel?* (Lake Mary, FL: Charisma House, 2018).
14. Terry Virgo, "Whatever Happened to the Promised Revival?," *Premier Christianity*, 2017.
15. R. T. Kendall, *Is God for the Homosexual?* (London: Marshall Pickering, 1988).

Chapter 7
Can We Know We Are Popular in Heaven?

1. R. T. Kendall, *Calvin and English Calvinism to 1649* (Great Britain: Paternoster, 1977).
2. For more information on the benefits of gratitude, see "In Praise of Gratitude," Harvard University, November 2011, https://www .health.harvard.edu/newsletter_article/in-praise-of-gratitude.
3. R. T. Kendall, *Just Say Thanks* (Lake Mary, FL: Charisma House, 2005).
4. Bible Gateway, s.v. "Proverbios 19:11," accessed May 31, 2018, https://www.biblegateway.com/passage/?search=pr.+19%3A11&version=LBLA.

Chapter 8
The World of Tartarus

1. Alexander Pope, "An Essay on Criticism," Poetry Foundation, accessed May 31, 2018, https://www.poetryfoundation.org/articles/69379/an-essay-on-criticism.
2. Bible Study Tools, s.v. "*Tartaroo*," accessed May 31, 2018, https://www.biblestudytools.com/lexicons/greek/nas/tartaroo.html.

Chapter 11
The Devil's Worst Nightmare

1. J. I. Packer, *Evangelism and the Sovereignty of God* (Downers Grove, IL: InterVarsity Press, 2009).
2. James S. Stewart, "The Rending of the Veil," Preaching Today, accessed June 2, 2018, http://www.preachingtoday.com/sermons/sermons/2006/march/rendingoftheveil.html.
3. Horatius Bonar, "Go, Labor On," Timeless Truths, accessed June 5, 2018, http://library.timelesstruths.org/music/Go_Labor_On/.

Chapter 12
Qualifications for Fame in Hell

1. William Cowper, "What Various Hindrances We Meet," accessed June 5, 2018, http://cyberhymnal.org/htm/w/v/wvhwmeet.htm.
2. "Billy Graham: I Know Where I'm Going," Beliefnet Inc., accessed June 5, 2018, http://www.beliefnet.com/columnists/news/2013/10/billy-graham-i-know-where-im-going.php.
3. Marian Anderson, "Crucifixion," YouTube video, posted by davidhertzberg, September 6, 2010, https://www.youtube.com/watch?v=A92bSnDmLYU.

Conclusion

1. "C. T. Studd Quotes," Goodreads Inc., accessed June 6, 2018, https://www.goodreads.com/quotes/243624-some-want-to-live-within-the-sound-of-church-or.

OTHER BOOKS BY R. T. KENDALL

40 Days With the Holy Spirit
By Love Transformed
Choosing Forgiveness
Controlling the Tongue
Did You Think to Pray?
Holy Fire
How to Forgive Ourselves—Totally
Imitating Christ
In Pursuit of His Wisdom
It Ain't Over Till It's Over
Grace
Jealousy
Just Say Thanks!
Pigeon Religion: Holy Spirit, Is That You?
Prepare Your Heart for the Midnight Cry
Pure Joy
The Anointing: Yesterday, Today, Tomorrow
The Power of Humility
The Presence of God
The Sensitivity of the Spirit
The Thorn in the Flesh
Totally Forgiving God
Whatever Happened to the Gospel?
When God Shows Up